Planning Profitable
New Product Strategies

An Alexander Hamilton Institute Book
Chilton's Better Business Series

Planning Profitable New Product Strategies

James W. Taylor

California State University, Fullerton

CHILTON BOOK COMPANY
RADNOR, PENNSYLVANIA

Copyright © 1982, 1984 by Alexander Hamilton Institute, Inc.
Modern Business Reports, 1633 Broadway, New York, NY 10019
All Rights Reserved
Published in Radnor, Pennsylvania 19089, by Chilton Book Company
Designed by Jean Callan King/Metier Industrial, Inc.
Manufactured in the United States of America

Library of Congress Cataloging in Publication Data
Taylor, James Walter, 1933–
    Planning profitable new product strategies.
    (Chilton's better business series)
    "An Alexander Hamilton Institute book."
    Includes index.
    1. New products.   I. Alexander Hamilton Institute (U.S.)
II. Title.   III. Series.
HF5414.153.T39   1984   658.5'75   84-1818
ISBN 0-8019-7522-0 (pbk.)

Chilton's Better Business Series
1 2 3 4 5 6 7 8 9 0   3 1 0 9 8 7 6 5 4

Contents

List of Figures

List of Tables

Introduction

No corporate function has a greater impact on the successful long-term growth of your company than new product development. "Planning Profitable New Product Strategies" contains everything you'll need to establish your own successful system.

This state-of-the-art guide covers each topic in the process in a practical and easy-to-understand manner. Sprinkled throughout the book are detailed actual examples and case histories which illustrate everything from Product Life Cycle analysis to new product idea generation to market testing procedures.

A unique and immediately usable feature of the report is the extensive Planning Pages which enable you to prepare your own:

- strengths and weaknesses rating chart
- served market definition sheet
- three-dimensional market structure
- items-by-use matrix
- Return On Investment summary sheet.

"Planning Profitable New Product Strategies" explains in depth the traditional tools and techniques in this area. In addition, you'll learn the latest in such sophisticated modern developments as perceptual mapping techniques for correctly positioning your product, and build-up estimating models for forecasting financial results.

After reading this comprehensive manual, you'll have a clear idea of how to:

- minimize costly new product projects that are doomed to fail
- refine your guidelines for decision-making in the new product area
- significantly increase the value of your new product system
- reduce the inherent risks in the product development process.

To provide you with this key information, we asked James W. Taylor, BBA, MBA, DBA, to compile pertinent material in conjunction with our own editors at the Alexander Hamilton Institute.

Dr. Taylor is currently a Professor at California State University, Fullerton, California. He has been intimately involved in marketing and new product development for more than 20 years as an educator, consultant and practicing executive.

He was formerly manager of Atlantic Refining Company's Research Division, Vice President of Economics Research Associates, and Director of New Product Development for Hunt-Wesson Foods, Inc.

Integrating the contents of this special report with your own unique talents and insights will product the best foundation possible for successful new product strategies in your company.

I

Why Develop New Products?

The first important point to understand about new product development is that a very large amount of money is being spent on it and it can be *very* expensive.

The second important point to understand clearly about new product development is that it is *very* risky. The general statistic for over 30 years in the U.S. has been that four of five new products fail. While this alarming statistic provides the "flavor" of the problem with new product development, it is somewhat misleading.

THE PROBLEM WITH STATISTICS

The first problem with that statistic is one of definition. What is a new product? Experts in the field of analyzing new product success and failure have great difficulty with this question. There is nothing even approaching a consensus on this point.

We will deal with this problem by defining it this way. A new product is defined as anything your company has not sold before. Note:

The word "product" will be used throughout this manual simply as a matter of convenience. If your company sells services, read "service" wherever "product" appears. Almost everything that applies to products also applies to services.

The second problem with the four out of five statistic is that it varies widely across industries, among companies and at various stages of the new product development process.

A SURVEY OF SUCCESS/FAILURE RATES

The Conference Board, a well-known business research organization headquartered in New York, conducted a survey in 1980 among medium and large-sized manufacturing firms in the United States regarding their experiences with new product introductions over the past five years. The Board found one metal components and equipment

SUCCESS* RATES FOR MAJOR NEW PRODUCTS IN PAST FIVE YEARS		
	Percent of Companies Selling Primarily to	
Percent of Successful New Products	Industrial Markets	Consumer Markets
All Succeeded	9%	18%
90 to 99%	7	4
80 to 89%	16	9
70 to 79%	11	11
60 to 69%	16	12
50 to 59%	15	15
40 to 49%	4	2
30 to 39%	9	9
1 to 29%	5	4
None Succeeded	8	16
	100%	100%

*Success was defined as meeting management's expectations in all important respects.

firm that introduced over 100 successful new products from 1974 to 1979 without a single failure. An electric components company had 25 successes and no failures; while one petroleum products firm had nine successes and no failures.

On the other hand, one chemical company had an unbroken string of 20 failures; a heating equipment firm reported 11 failures and no successes; and a sporting goods manufacturer has six failures without a success.

Another important concept to understand about new product development is that it *can be* a high risk business activity. *But* it doesn't always have to be. This manual will show you how to reduce the inherent risk in new product development to acceptable levels.

WHY DO YOU NEED NEW PRODUCTS?

If new product development is such an expensive and risky undertaking, a reasonable question for an executive to ask is, "Why should we develop new products?" There are several good answers to that question. One is profit. Consider these examples.

The SmithKline Corporation is a pharmaceutical products company headquartered in Philadelphia, Pennsylvania. In 1976, SmithKline introduced a new product in the United Kingdom followed a year later by introduction in the U.S. The new product was an ulcer remedy called Tagamet. The drug actually heals peptic ulcers. Tagamet is now sold in over one hundred countries around the world. It is one of the most remarkable successes of the 1970's.

By 1979, SmithKline's revenues reached $1.35 billion—a gain of 129% over 1975, the year before Tagamet was introduced. Profits in 1979 came to $234 million, a 266% increase over the four-year period. Tagamet accounted for more than a third of the entire company's sales and about half of its profits.

By 1980, Tagamet's worldwide sales were $649,000,000—more than the entire company's total sales before Tagamet.

SmithKline is a very old, well-established company. Activision, Inc. is a very young company, founded in 1979 in Santa Clara, California. Activision manufactures and sells videogame cartridges for use in home video game systems. These systems hook into a television set and produce a colorful display on the screen that players can manipulate to hit a tennis ball, play soccer or shoot down an alien space ship, for example.

During 1980, Activision's first full year in operation, the company sold over five million units at just over $10 per unit to record revenues in excess of $50 million.

The company is privately held and does not disclose earnings, but informed estimates place Activision's 1980 *after tax* income at $8 to $10 million.

In 1980, Activision forecasts sales of over $150 million and an even greater profit margin. All of this was accomplished on an investment of less than $1 million.

In 1977 in Melbourne, Australia, the Victorian Dairy Industry Authority was facing a combination of slow population growth and declining per capita consumption of the dairy industry's most profitable product, milk. In the Australian state of Victoria per capita consumption of milk had dropped from 0.385 liters in 1960 to 0.327 liters in 1976. This long-term, steady erosion prompted the government to create the Authority in 1976 to represent the interests of the state's twenty-three independent dairy companies.

At the same time, per capita consumption of soft drinks in 1976 stood at 78 liters. The Victorian Dairy Industry Authority turned to new product development aimed directly at soft drinks. It developed a line of flavored milk in individual serving packages that did not require refrigeration. It called the line "Big M."

Twelve months after its introduction, Big M had captured an estimated 10% of the entire non-alcoholic beverage market. Big M accounted for 13% of total milk sales which, in turn, were up 7%. Big M generated over $3 million in its first year on the market.

WHAT HAPPENS IF YOU DON'T DEVELOP NEW PRODUCTS?

The most likely answer to that question is, "Nothing." At least not right away. But that's the problem. Virtually no company is in business just for the short term. So it is instructive to look at the long-term performance of some companies that did *not* develop new products.

The Fotomat Corporation is based in Wilton, Connecticut and operates or franchises about 3,700 retail outlets that sell film processing services, photographic film and accessories. Most of the company's stores are free-standing kiosks which utilize the "drive-through" concept. These stores are located in high traffic sites, such as shopping centers, in metropolitan and suburban areas throughout the U.S. Fotomat's sales and profits during the past ten years are shown in the box.

(Million $)			
Year Ended	Net Sales	Operating Income	Net Income
1980	235	11.8	(1.8)
1979	206	10.5	(4.69)
1978	190	21.6	6.30
1977	177	25.6	9.86
1976	144	22.4	9.84
1975	119	19.0	8.17
1974	88	11.6	3.40
1973	63	6.9	1.71
1972	45	2.7	Nil
1971	44	(2.3)	(3.28)

Founded in 1966, Fotomat grew very nicely for the first 10 years of its existence by continually opening more stores. During this period, Fotomat added no new products and ignored two significant changes in the market; 1) the rapid increase in sales of 35mm cameras and film, which it did not sell, and 2) the rapid growth in sales of home video recorders.

As a result, Fotomat was in a very poor position to deal with a sharp increase in film prices, reduced driving caused by energy problems, and simply running out of good new locations for expansion. Fotomat has since corrected these mistakes.

While Fotomat was a young company that grew rapidly while ignoring the need for new products, Hoover Universal, Inc. is an established company that was content to rely on the industrial products growth of its customers to fuel its own growth.

This Ann Arbor, Michigan-based diversified company is involved in the automotive, shelter, packaging, plastics working machinery, and general industrial markets. It is the largest noncaptive producer of automotive seating with about 50% of the total market. Hoover's record for the 1970's is in the following box.

(Million $)			
Year Ended	Net Sales	Operating Income	Net Income
1980	573	59.6	19.4
1979	601	73.0	31.5
1978	498	61.8	29.3
1977	415	58.6	25.9
1976	328	52.3	18.1
1975	271	36.7	11.7
1974	256	29.0	10.7
1973	259	36.2	13.7
1972	221	30.7	11.3
1971	176	22.0	7.2

Twice during that period, in 1974 and again in 1980, Hoover's business was battered by the misfortunes of the U.S. auto industry.

In the mid-70's, Hoover did venture into the plastic beverage bottle market. But this division has yet to make a profit.

Hoover has a new management that is rapidly building up its new product development capability. For the first time it is seriously searching for ways to separate itself from the automobile business.

ANOTHER CASE OF LACK OF NEW PRODUCT DEVELOPMENT

AM International (formerly known as Addressograph-Multigraph) is an exceptionally interesting case that illustrates all three of our points. Namely, 1) revenues and earnings can be threatened without new products, 2) new product development is risky, and 3) it is expensive.

For many years, AM was a marginally profitable manufacturer of old-fashioned duplicators and addressing machines. Its management did not react at first as xerographic copiers made in the U.S. and Japan took over AM's market.

In 1976, the Board of Directors elected a new Chairman who promptly replaced 80% of the old management and radically altered the company's product structure. Some of the new products that AM began to develop included word processors, small office computers, microfilm and microfiche equipment, credit card data recording equipment, and point of sale recording systems. AM International results appear in the box below.

(Million $)			
Year Ended	Net Sales	Operating Income	Net Income
1980	910	28.6	4.0
1979	754	33.8	9.0
1978	667	57.6	21.3
1977	596	37.9	(14.0)
1976	593	36.7	6.4
1975	584	37.0	4.9
1974	541	24.9	0.3
1973	490	34.1	3.2
1972	436	41.4	16.7
1971	412	41.9	5.0

By 1981, AM's sales dropped to $857 million on which it lost a staggering $245 million. AM's equity dropped to $14 million in 1981 from $232 million in 1980. At this point, AM International prepared to file for bankruptcy.

AM International is a case of what can happen to a company that does not have a *consistent* policy to develop new products. It also points out what can happen to a company that fails to control its new product development activity. This manual will help you avoid both pitfalls.

II

Initiating the Thought Process Behind New Product Development Strategy

It is clear that the primary aims of new product development are to increase sales revenues and. more importantly, to increase profits.

While accomplishing both those tasks is vital to every business, new product development is not the only way to do it. The "Opportunities Matrix" in Table 1 is a widely-used method designed to help you organize your thinking on new products.

	Existing Products	New Products
Existing Markets	Quadrant I	Quadrant III
New Markets	Quadrant II	Quadrant IV

Table 1. A simplified Opportunities Matrix

When you look at the growth opportunities for your business in this way, four possible areas of activity emerge.

Think about how you actually make your business grow. You take today's profits and invest them in your business, expecting to generate a greater future return than if you had invested them in a bank account or some other financial instrument.

FORECASTING YOUR GROWTH

Try this exercise. Refer to your business plan to make a rough estimate of what amount of your sales and profits you'd like five years from now.

Total Revenues Five Years From Now _____.

Total Profits Five Years From Now _____

Now make a list of all the projects that you could undertake in the next five years to make your business grow by selling more of your existing products in your existing markets (Quadrant I). Then estimate the total sales revenues that you could reasonably expect each project to produce in the fifth year. Do the same thing for profits from each of those projects. Use Table 2 to record your estimates.

Next, turn your attention to Quadrant II and make a list of the *new markets* in which you might reasonably expect to sell your existing products in the next five years. Consider geographical expansion and export markets. List those opportunities and your estimates of fifth year sales and profits in Table 3.

Think about what your sales revenues and profits are most likely to be in five years if you *don't* do any of these projects. Write those numbers below.

Fifth Year Sales Revenue
  With No New Projects   _____
Fifth Year Profits With No
  New Projects   _____

Now combine your estimates and compare the totals with where you said you would like to be in five years.

	SALES REVENUES	PROFITS
Assuming No New Projects	_____	_____
Existing Products in Existing Markets	_____	_____
Existing Products in New Markets	_____	_____
Total	_____	_____

If the totals are as large, or larger, than your fifth year goals you are in good shape. You have lots of work to do in the areas you know best where your chances for success are highest. They are also the least expensive areas in which to make your business grow because you are utilizing existing plant, equipment, personnel, etc.

Projects Involving Existing Products in Existing Markets	Fifth Year Sales Revenue	Fifth Year Profits
_____	_____	_____
_____	_____	_____
_____	_____	_____
_____	_____	_____
_____	_____	_____
_____	_____	_____
_____	_____	_____

Table 2. Sales and profits estimates for existing markets

Projects Involving Existing Products in New Markets	Fifth Year Sales Revenue	Fifth Year Profits
_____	_____	_____
_____	_____	_____
_____	_____	_____
_____	_____	_____
_____	_____	_____
_____	_____	_____
_____	_____	_____
_____	_____	_____

Table 3. Sales and profits estimates for new markets

However, remember that all those numbers are based on certain assumptions about what will happen, or won't happen. Further, you may not have carefully examined all those assumptions.

ANALYZING TECHNOLOGY

You have probably made your estimates on the assumption that the technology in your industry won't change much in the next five years. How good an assumption is that?

In 1981, SONY announced that it was developing a camera that looks like a regular 35mm camera but that records images on a video-disc instead of conventional film. The impact of such new technology on every business related to photography would be profound.

What will happen to the companies that supply the basic chemicals to the film manufacturers? What are the implications for the management at Fotomat? What kinds of changes are likely for major customers of photographs, such as newspapers and magazines?

Give serious thought to the likelihood of significant technological change in your industry and in your customers' industries, especially if you sell industrial products. What are the chances that there will not be significant technological changes in the next five years? Do it on a percentage basis. 100% means you are certain that there will be major changes and 0% means there is no chance of anything changing. Record it below.

The probability of major technological changes in the next five years _____%

CONSIDERING INVENTIONS

Recent research demonstrates that throughout the 20th century, the majority of the major technological threats to established industries came from outside those industries.

Suppose that you had worked for a Swiss watch manufacturer in 1969. Do you suppose you would have been aware that, on the other side of the world, Japanese technicans were working on LED (Light Emitting Diode) technology to make meters easier to read? Even if you were aware of their efforrts, could you have had any idea of the devastating impact that work would have on the Swiss watch industry during the 1970's?

It is a difficult, but important, effort to judge the threat of technological change from *outside* your industry. Use the same percentage basis.

The probability of major technological changes from *outside* in the next five years _____%

STUDYING REGULATIONS

Everywhere in the world, government action is increasingly a factor in business activity. How sure are you that the government won't take some action that could have a major impact on your existing business? It doesn't even have to be your own government.

The Dresdner Bank of the Federal Republic of Germany learned that lesson in 1981 as the lead bank in the group that lent Poland some $13.5 billion dollars prior to the declaration of martial law in that country.

It is not just the areas that governments start to regulate. It is also those things they stop doing. When President Carter signed the law de-regulating the U.S. air carrier industry, he produced shock waves that will be felt in that industry for at least a decade.

The probability of major new government regulation, or de-regulation, in your industry in the next five years _____%

ANALYZING RAW MATERIAL COSTS AND AVAILABILITY

Your estimates of your future sales were based on certain assumptions about price levels. Those pricing assumptions, in turn, were based on other assumptions about how the prices of your raw materials would behave.

The sharply higher world prices for coffee in the mid-1970's led to sharp declines in per capita consumption of coffee in the U.S. Virtually everyone has some favorite piece of gold or silver jewelry that increased in value dramatically at some point. But the major use of these precious metals is in manufacturing, not in jewelry. The rapid increase in silver prices at one time produced price increases of 50 to 150% in film, as an example.

With price increases for raw materials, you at least have the possibility of passing them through to your customer. But if the raw materials are simply not available, it is quite a different situation. The shortage of peanuts in 1980–81 caused a number of brands of peanut butter to disappear from the shelves of supermarkets.

The probability that your raw materials will be affected by some major change in prices or availability in the next five years _____%

YOUR CHANGING CUSTOMER BASE

One very significant assumption concerns your customers. The most usual assumption is that they won't change much at all. Or if they do, it will be slowly and in a direction that is easy to detect.

In most cases, nothing could be further from the truth. Not only are customers likely to change, but it is frequently difficult to understand what those changes mean to the products of individual companies.

Just understanding straightforward demographic trends can be extremely difficult. For example, between 1970 and 1980 the population of the U.S. grew 9%. But the number of households grew 26%.

That means there are a lot more one and two person households. But exactly what are the implications for the manufacturers of washing machines? For the producers of large economy size detergents? For processors of frozen foods? For the makers of sheets and pillow cases?

This example only considers the fact that people are rapidly rearranging their living configurations. It doesn't question the changes in attitudes and values that have led to these demographic changes. It's those changes in attitudes and values that most often have the real impact on the demand for goods and services.

Even if you make industrial products, it is not likely that you are completely isolated from such changes. In the end, the demand for your customers' products, or your customers' customers' products, is derived from the demands of consumers.

The probability that there will be a significant change in your customer base in the next five years _____%

DO YOU NEED NEW PRODUCTS

If your five year sales and profits estimates met your five year goals— and all your probability estimates were in the 0% to 10% range—then you can logically conclude that new product development is not a very important function for the growth and health of your business.

You will also have the comfort of knowing that you are in a very rare business. So rare that you might want to go back and double check your estimates.

OTHER WAYS TO MAKE YOUR BUSINESS GROW

Look back at the Opportunities Matrix in Table 1. You can see that when you are managing your existing products in your existing markets and in all possible new markets as well as you possibly can, then additional growth *must* come from developing new products or services. There is no other possibility.

In Quadrant III, new products for existing markets, you will primarily address internal development of new products. In Quadrant IV, new products for new markets, you have the choice of internal development or acquisition. You should always measure new product development program costs against the cost of getting similar dollars of sales and profits from acquisitions. A number of very successful organizations have been built almost completely on carefully planned and executed acquisitions.

III

Using the Product Life Cycle as a Marketing Development Tool

The fundamental, underlying mechanism that gives importance to new product development can be found in the Product Life Cycle (PLC). While the PLC is a theory and can never be proven experimentally, it is a useful theory in the way Kenneth Boulding, the noted economist, meant when he remarked, "There is nothing quite so useful as a theory that works."

Basically, the PLC uses a biological analogy to suggest that every product passes through a regular sequence of events, or stages, beginning with conception, followed by birth, growth, maturity and finally, decline. Table 4 shows the usual manner in which the product life cycle is displayed.

THE PLC AS A BUSINESS TOOL

The great value of the PLC as a business planning tool is that it relates product sales to time in a logical, systematic manner. In addition, there

Biological Phase	Business Stage
Conception	New Product Development
Birth	Market Introduction
Growth	Market Expansion
Adolescence	Market Turbulence
Maturity	Market Saturation
Old Age	Market Decline

Table 4. The biological-business analogy of the PLC

are strong patterns of price, cost, distribution and competitive behavior associated with each of the stages of the PLC. If you can locate where your products currently are on the PLC, you have a reasonable basis for anticipating future developments.

Although the Product Life Cycle can never be verified experimentally, researchers have demonstrated its existence in thousands of product categories in countries throughout the world. PLC's have been observed in consumer disposables, such as instant coffee, consumer durables, such as sewing machines, high technology products, like optical scanning systems, and industrial products, from capital goods to office supplies.

Exceptions to the general form exist. For example, prescription drugs tend to display a double cycle. The second cycle coincides with the end of the traditional 17-year patent protection. At that time, the original manufacturer frequently increases promotion sharply to protect his position. New competitors enter the market with low cost generic versions of the original. This combination frequently causes a second Market Expansion stage.

There are also problems involved with specifying the market and in measurement. But the PLC remains a valuable tool for organizing and focusing your thinking and strategy, and anticipating the future.

USING THE PLC

Understanding where your business fits on the PLC is useful in two ways. It will help you organize your thinking about where your various products are in terms of their individual life cycles. You can then concentrate your new product development activities in those product areas where you currently have mature products and are most vulnerable.

It will also help you anticipate which of your present products are likely to require large amounts of cash in the future. Since new product development is expensive, there is little point in starting projects that may well have to be halted due to lack of funds.

ANALYZING THE VARIOUS STAGES IN THE PLC

The entire process begins with product development, a time of considerable uncertainty. Expenses may be high and only rarely will there be any income (an exception might be a government-sponsored project).

This manual addresses that phase and helps you deal with the inevitable uncertainty in a systematic manner, while implementing the most efficient cost control procedures. To the extent that you are successful in this activity, new products will be introduced to the market. At that point the observable PLC begins.

MARKET INTRODUCTION STAGE

When new products first reach the market, unit prices are usually high primarily because costs are high. Manufacturing costs are high because:

- runs are short
- the manufacturing department is not yet certain what the most efficient production methods are
- engineering is not certain what the best materials are
- purchasing has not yet located the lowest cost suppliers.

Marketing costs are high because:

- the sales department is not quite sure how to sell the product
- advertising the promotion are inefficient since the best pros-pects are difficult to identify and locate
- distributors demand high margins to offset their inventory investment risk.

You objective in the market place is to generate trial purchases for your new product. High product quality is particularly important during the Market Introduction Stage because you are attempting to build a base for future growth.

Sales will be low, but at least some cash will begin to flow into the company. Sales growth will most likely be slow because you are attempting to change basic behavior patterns.

Revenue generating is not the most important consideration in this phase. The most important activity in the Market Development Stage is *learning*. You need to find:

- What product configuration is most in demand
- Who the best customers are
- How customers actually use the new product
- How they perceive the product's benefits
- How to best distribute the product.

ADJUSTING TO THE MARKET PLACE

The really big investments in manufacturing and marketing usually develop later. It is imperative that you learn how to best adjust all of your market place activities before the market takes off and starts to grow. This is the single best way to ensure that your company has a strong and profitable position in the market as it develops.

It is also important to learn as early as possible if there is no demand, and if the cause was a bad idea or bad execution.

In the 1960's, DuPont introduced an imitation leather product called Corfam that was intended to penetrate the manufacturing of shoes. Corfam never got out of the Market Introduction Stage.

When DuPont finally abandoned the product, its losses were variously estimated at between $80 and $100 million. While there are a lot of opinions about what went wrong, the fundamental problem was that DuPont failed to learn that consumers will not accept shoes that do not "breathe"—and Corfam did not breathe.

How much DuPont might have saved if it had concentrated on *learning* rather than *sales generating* is impossible to say. However, the lesson is apparent.

At some point, if it ever happens, forces in the market place will come together and demand for the new product will begin to grow rapidly. Then the Market Expansion Stage begins.

MARKET EXPANSION STAGE

The signal for this stage is a continuing upsurge in sales accompanied by a strong increase in manufacturing budgets and marketing budgets. That is why the greatest total financial risks often occur in the Market Expansion Stage.

The offsetting factor is that now there is a strong cash flow. The question of when some of this cash flow becomes profit is highly dependent on how well you planned for the increased sales and how well you control the rapid growth.

The first significant change in the market when a product enters the Market Expansion Stage is most likely an increase in the number of competitors.

A rapid growth rate and an apparent large final market will attract proportionately more large firms. While the exact nature of the newly emerging competitive structure is unknowable, the fact that it will be there is unquestionable.

MEETING THE COMPETITION

During the Market Introduction Stage, it was sufficient just to get a customer to make a purchase in the product category. During Market Expansion, it becomes extremely important for you to define and defend one or more market segments for yourself. This is the time when major improvements in the basic product are likely to be introduced.

Potential new competitors study the market to find segments with unmet needs, design a product to meet those needs, and use that new design as the reason customers should buy from them.

There is even evidence among consumer packaged goods products that the more competitors who enter the market, the faster the total market grows. That's when the market leader's share grows the fastest, one of the real rewards of early entry.

What happens is the total advertising and promotion for the product category grows more rapidly than distribution. A customer sees or hears Company 5's advertising, but finds available only the products of Company 1, Company 2 and Company 3. So while Company 5 "created" the new customer, someone else gets the purchase.

Along with increased competition, rapid sales growth induces rapidly expanding distribution. Wholesalers and retailers see, or think they see, new profit opportunities for themselves in the emerging market. This increasing availability of the new product in turn fuels sales growth.

This is the time when prices begin to come down. Part of the reason for this behavior is that costs begin to come down with increased production and marketing experience.

Along with falling variable per unit costs, fixed costs come down as a percent of unit costs. You simply have a much larger base to spread fixed costs over. Some of these cost improvements will be taken as profits. But frequently some are passed on to customers in the form of lower prices to strengthen the company's position and to avoid holding out a "price umbrella" which might entice even more new competitors to enter the market.

MARKET TURBULENCE STAGE

At some point, the market will begin to approach its upper limit, and growth will continue at a lower rate than previously. When this happens, it puts severe pressures on the weaker members of the industry. Some manufacturers will recognize that they have failed to establish a satisfactory position in the new market and drop out. They may, however, sell off inventories at sharply reduced prices which will produce some temporary price pressures in the industry.

Other members may not be so orderly in their actions. Either through faulty analysis or because they over-invested in the new business, they may decide that they must stay at all costs.

The invariable reaction is to try to "buy" a position in the business. The first price cuts will tend to be deep, on large quantities and out of sight of the market. Special deals on a rail car quantity of merchandise to some selected customers is one example. These price reductions are extremely difficult to verify and it is thus difficult to formulate an appropriate reaction.

You'll find formerly good customers suddenly order substantially reduced quantities, or greatly stretch out their order intervals. Once the price cuts become common knowledge, you may have little choice except to reduce profits and/or volume until the "shake-out" is completed.

DERIVING SOME POSITIVES FROM THIS STAGE

While the Market Turbulence Stage may contain many perils, there is also the possibility for some good events to occur. You may be able to acquire plant or equipment in good condition at bargain prices. The same is also true of packaging or raw materials. You may also be able to gain some important new distribution capacities.

During this period you need exceptional sensitivity to what is happening to the market and to your competitors, considerable flexibility to take advantage of such opportunities, and above all, the ability to make speedy decisions.

Market Turbulence is a time when manufacturers tend to introduce higher levels of service as a non-price method of competing. If you have anticipated this development, you can avoid much of these usually expensive and ineffective service programs.

MARKET SATURATION STAGE

When this stage is reached, demand still grows, but in response to some secondary characteristic rather than to the original market expansion demand. Color television set sales in the U.S. now grow primarily in response to new household formations. Industrial products sales that respond to equipment wearout are another example.

The surviving competitors will be approximately in place and the industry will move toward a position of competitive equilibrium. Competitive equilibrium usually occurs when the competitors have arranged themselves so that a size ratio of approximately 0.6 is attained. That is, when the second largest company has sales about 60% the size of the market leader, and so on. Recent research on over 1,200 companies in mature markets produced these results:

POSITION	AVERAGE SHARE OF MARKET
Leader	33%
Second largest	19%
Third largest	12%
Fourth largest	7%

You can also anticipate that the largest market share company will be the most profitable. Here are the profit levels on the companies shown above:

	FOUR YEAR AVERAGE
	PRE-TAX RETURN ON
MARKET SHARE	INVESTMENT
Over 40%	32.3%
30 to 40%	24.4
20 to 30%	23.6
10 to 20%	18.0
Under 10%	13.2

These differences in profitability trace quite directly to lower costs, especially marketing costs, for the larger share companies.

The message that comes out of all of this is that market share is profitable. Getting market share during the Market Saturation Stage is expensive, because the only place to get new business is from competitors who are unlikely to give it up easily.

There is one time, however, when it is relatively *inexpensive* to gain market share. That is during Market Expansion. At that time, you can build market share by gaining larger proportions of *new* customers coming into the market place. Market share is most profitable when it is acquired during the Market Expansion Stage. That is why companies invest in new product development. They hope to be able to create new markets.

MARKET DECLINE STAGE

Eventually total industry sales will start to decline. If you are currently selling products in markets that are visibly declining, you *know* you *need* new products.

EVALUATING THE SHORTENED DURATION OF PLCS

Very strong evidence exists that in at least one area of business (see Table 5), new products are reaching the Market Saturation Stage in shorter and shorter periods of time. To the extent that this trend holds true for other areas of business, two implications should concern you.

One is that the shrinking time period between when the first new product appears on the market and when the entire product category reaches maturity leaves less and less time to adjust new product offerings in the market place. That places increasing importance on improving the new product development process *before* the product reaches the market.

The other implication is that if you do not have an on-going new product development program in your company and any of your competitors do, the time available for you to respond to their new products is rapidly shrinking.

INCORPORATING THE PLC CONCEPT IN YOUR STRATEGY

Each company executive must tailor the way he uses the PLC concept to the situation and needs of his own company. After you consider the type of products you have, the needs of your market, and your projections for the future (Section II), you'll be in a good position to utilize the following Planning Pages.

Planning Pages 1 and 2 will help you get started. Each is a worksheet for the same product. Make copies if you need more. Each page approaches the PLC in a different way. Product Planning Page 1 allows you to attempt to develop mathematical descriptions of your PLCs. A useful characteristic of the PLC is that the boundary between each stage is an inflection point, that is, *a point where the rate of change changes*.

Ideally, you will be able to identify such inflection points by carefully examining the rate at which the total category for each of your products has been changing.

For example, the world market for mobile telephones grew at a single digit rate for much of the 1970's. 1981 seems to have marked an inflection point between Market Introduction and Market Expansion. Growth rates of 20% to 28% are expected for much of the 1980's. Eventually, the market for mobile telephones will begin to approach saturation and a 20% or better growth rate will no longer be sustainable. At that time, another inflection point will appear and the *growth rate* will begin to fall back.

People who work in new product development frequently remark that the length of the PLC is continually growing shorter, that products seem to move through stages faster. Since this kind of impression is very hard to verify or to disprove, the results of recent research into this question are interesting.

The researchers studied thirty-seven household appliances introduced into the U.S. market some time between 1922 and 1979. They then divided the products into three groups. The first group included those products introduced prior to World War I (1922–1942). This group of twelve products included clothes washers, hot plates, toasters, etc.

The second group of sixteen products were introduced after World War II (1945–1964). This group included such items as air conditioners, can openers, dishwashers and black and white television sets. The third group of nine products were introduced between 1965 and 1979. Included in this group were automatic coffeemakers, curling irons, hair dryers and color television sets.

The researchers studied factory shipments to determine the length of time each product category was in each stage of PLC. Although there are wide ranges for individual products within each group, the mean values in time for each group are of considerable interest.

AVERAGE NUMBER OF YEARS NEW U.S. HOUSEHOLD APPLIANCES REMAINED IN STAGES OF THE PLC

PRODUCT GROUP	MARKET INTRODUCTION STAGE	MARKET EXPANSION STAGE
Group I (1922–1942)	12.5	33.8
Group II (1945–1964)	7.0	19.5
Group III (1965–1979)	2.0	6.8

Further, if you exclude just one item, color television sets, from Group III the values become even smaller; 0.9 years for the Market Introduction Stage and 5.7 years for the Market Expansion Stage.

Table 5. Research on shortened Product Life Cycles

FILLING OUT PLANNING PAGES

Examine the right hand column on Part One carefully to identify inflection points after filling in the first two columns. You may need to "smooth" these data to see what is happening more clearly. Use a moving average, or plot the data on a graph and try to fit a curve to it.

Part Two (Figure 2) of the Planning Pages approaches the task from a judgment basis. The major characteristics of each stage of the PLC are listed along with the PLC stages. Mark the characteristics of each of your product categories by circling the "X" that indicates the best description of each characteristic. (Note: some will have two X's. Circle both of them).

For example, the price of pocket size audio receivers ("pagers" or "beepers") has fallen from $300 to $150 in the past few years. That is definitely a characteristic of the Market Expansion Stage.

When you have completed this page, you should be able to study the columns and indentify the appropriate stage through the predominance of circled X's. The pattern may not be perfect, but the real world doesn't always conform to judgments or mathematical formulas.

The best result is when both Part One and Part Two give you the same answer. If they don't, examine all of the parts carefully and try to determine why you are getting conflicting answers.

Study these plotted data. Then using what you know is likely to happen at each stage of the product life cycle, take a separate sheet of paper. Begin a list of the kinds of things that can happen to your company in the future. Pay particular attention to products in the Market Saturation or Market Decline Stages. What you can do to replace them is a good starting point for thinking about new product development.

THE ISSUE OF WHAT INDUSTRY LEVEL TO USE

One issue in PLC analysis that will require special thought and judgment is the industry level of aggregation to use. Should you use the generic product class, the product form or the brand detail?

By way of example, do you study integrated circuits (chips), or 64K RAM's (Random Access Memory)? Or do you study Motorola's sales of 64K RAM's?

PRODUCT LIFE CYCLE IDENTIFICATION—PART ONE

YEAR	TOTAL PRODUCT CATEGORY SALES	PERCENT CHANGE OVER PREVIOUS YEAR	ABSOLUTE PERCENTAGE POINT CHANGE FROM PREVIOUS YEAR
19__	_____	Not applicable	Not applicable
19__	_____	_____	_____
19__	_____	_____	_____
19__	_____	_____	_____
19__	_____	_____	_____
19__	_____	_____	_____
19__	_____	_____	_____
19__	_____	_____	_____
19__	_____	_____	_____
19__	_____	_____	_____
19__	_____	_____	_____
19__	_____	_____	_____
19__	_____	_____	_____

How The Product Category Was Defined:

_____

_____

Figure 1. Identifying inflection points for a product

Product Planning Page 2

Product Life Cycle Identification - Part Two

Market Characteristics	Stage In Product Life Cycle				
	Intro	Expan	Turb	Satur	Decline
Total Category Sales					
Growing slowly	X			X	
Growing rapidly		X			
Slowing down			X		
Declining					X
Number of New Competitors					
A few	X				
Many		X			
None of any importance				X	
Actually fewer			X		
Prices (In constant dollars)					
Stable	X			X	X
Declining		X			
Erratic			X		
Total Number of Items Available for Sale					
Increasing		X			
No real change	X			X	
Decreasing			X		X
Distribution Levels					
Expanding slowly	X				
Expanding rapidly		X			
Pretty stable				X	
Declining			X		X
Number of Recent Major Product Changes					
Few	X			X	
Many		X			
None of any importance				X	X
Basic Message Content of Most of the Advertising and/or Sales Literature					
Basic benefits	X				
Major product features		X	X		
Secondary characteristics (i.e., colors, sizes, etc.)				X	
New uses					X

Figure 2. Judging the stage of your product on the PLC

Evidence suggests that the PLC doesn't show very much at the brand level unless the brand really dominates the market. At the other extreme, the generic product class is usually so broad that individual segments can behave quite differently within it.

For instance, world semiconductor sales are expected to grow modestly between now and 1985. But 64K RAM's are expected to grow from the present $100 million sales level to $2 billion by 1985.

Generally, product form is the most usable level of aggregation. But you must give it special consideration.

OTHER DIFFICULT ISSUES

How to combine the product form with the market correctly is another issue you'll have to resolve. An example would be a shock absorber manufacturer who sold his products both to automobile manufacturers and to independent auto supply stores. There are clearly two product-market combinations here that have to be treated separately. Other times it is not so easy to identify the combination.

What product forms to aggregate is another issue. Suppose the shock absorber manufacturer sells automobile manufacturers a line of heavy duty absorbers for trucks and a line of medium duty absorbers for passenger cars. Should the two lines be treated separately? Further, suppose the company has international sales. Should every country be treated separately?

There are no simple answers to the questions raised by these issues. The best advice is to analyze very carefully and to try different approaches and combinations. In the end you will have to rely on your own good judgment.

SOME FINAL ADVICE

Make every possible effort to work with data in physical units. Inflation causes incredible distortions. If it is impossible to avoid using monetary measures, you will have to find a way to turn them into constant units.

Most countries produce some measurement similar to the United States' Gross National Product Deflator. If you are in doubt, ask your banker for assistance. It's his business to know what money is really worth.

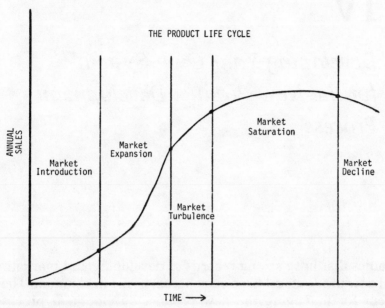

THE PRODUCT LIFE CYCLE

The product life cycle

IV

Developing Your Own System for the New Product Development Process

Companies that have strong records of developing and marketing successful new products all have one characteristic in common. They have a system for managing the new product development process. The details of how those systems work vary widely in response to industry and company differences. But most of the systems have similar underlying structures, or processes, for the development.

INCORPORATING THE BEST ASPECTS INTO YOUR SYSTEM

If your company is to become a successful developer of new products or improve its current success rate, you'll have to a) implement the fundamentals of the process and then b) find methods to make the individual parts of the process suitable for operation in your own company and in your own industry.

This Section provides you with an overall view of the successful new product development process. It also examines the most important pragmatic considerations involved in adopting the process.

Subsequent Sections follow each step in the process and offer a collection of methods, activities, procedures, and tools which companies have found useful in dealing with problems inherent in each step of the process.

You will have to select the individual tools that make sense for your company and try them. Some won't work and should be abandoned. Others will require adaptation to fit your needs.

In the end, you will have taken the "skeleton" of the process and added the features and details that are specific to your own organization.

Through trial and error, you will create a new product development system that works for you. No one can give you a detailed blueprint that will describe exactly how that unique system will turn out. But the remaining Sections will give you a lot of ideas to work with and suggestions for avoiding common pitfalls.

WHY HAVE A NEW PRODUCT DEVELOPMENT PROCESS?

Everyone has a favorite story about how somebody got a flash of inspiration and turned it into a multi-million dollar business. It happens. But the "stroke of genius" method of new product development is fatally flawed as a strategy for an on-going business. It is unpredictable and uncontrollable, and therefore unmanageable. You can't build a long-term business on unmanageable activities.

That is the reason that the new product development process has come into existence. While the process is not completely predictable or completely controllable, it is manageable. It is a business activity that responds to the application of skill and experience by managers.

Every successful new product development process has the following seven elements, although the details and emphases will vary.

GUIDELINES FOR SEARCHING

Suppose someone walked into your office today and said they had solved all the problems for making an atomic powered airplane. He then asked if you were interested in building one. Your most likely answer would be "no."

Your reason would be "that's not the business we're in," or "that's not the business we want to be in." That is exactly the reason you must establish guidelines. You must decide in advance what business you are in and what business or businesses you want to be in. Guidelines provide a focus to your search for new opportunities.

PROMOTING IDEA GENERATION

You must have methods for generating lots of new ideas. The internationally-known management consulting firm, Booz, Allen & Hamilton, Inc., conducted a study of 51 companies with good new product development records. It found that an average of 58 new ideas was required to produce *one* successful new product.

It is useful to think of this phenomenon as an idea decay curve,

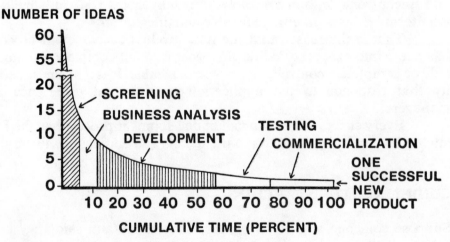

NEW PRODUCT IDEA DECAY CURVE
(58 NEW PRODUCT IDEAS — 51 COMPANIES)

Figure 3. A graphic depiction of the idea decay curve

as pictured in Figure 3. Things that can happen to an idea along the way to becoming a successful new product are:

- The ideas originally generated don't meet the guidelines
- They don't generate big enough markets
- They turn out not to be technically feasible so they end up not delivering the desired benefit
- Or they fail to achieve sufficient distribution when the products are introduced.

SCREENING CONCEPTS

As your methods for generating ideas begin to work, they will produce some concepts with excellent potential, some with average potential and some with poor potential. You will need a simple, fast, and inexpensive system to sort out those ideas.

You need a screening procedure that eliminates the concepts with poor or average potential, and lets those with superior potential go further. This procedure must balance the requirement of being simple and quick against the risk of turning down a really good idea. It must be inexpensive, both in terms of time and money, so you can concentrate the bulk of your resources on the few product concepts that appear to hold the most potential.

CONDUCTING BUSINESS ANALYSIS

There must be a systematic method to evaluate the business opportunity represented by each idea that passes the screening test. Among other questions you'll need to answer are:

- How big might the market be?
- How feasible is technical development?
- What would our prices be? Our costs?
- What are the chances of success?

While all the steps in the new product development are crucial, business analysis is the point at which you make decisions about which new product concepts to invest in, which new product concepts *not* to invest in, and on what timetable these investments will be made.

Everything that happens thereafter in the process is established by the business analysis step. If strong concepts are selected, everything else that remains to be done gets easier and success becomes more likely. Conversely, weak concepts make everything more difficult and success less likely. And if strong concepts are overlooked, important opportunities are lost, probably forever.

DEVELOPING PROTOTYPES

After funds have been designated to support specific new product concepts, you need a system to develop prototypes. Prototypes must be developed for both the product concept *and* the communication to the market.

A successful new product delivers important benefits to prospective customers. Prototype development provides firm answers to two questions. First, whether the proposed benefit can be communicated in a clear and meaningful way to the target market. Second, whether the new product is likely to deliver the benefit promised.

The decisions made at the prototype development stage are major money decisions because they involve building pilot plants or investing in other hard assets. Decisions up to this point have basically been profit and loss decisions, that is, their impact is limited primarily to the company profit and loss statement.

Decisions to move beyond the prototype stage begin to reach the level of balance sheet decisions. Balance sheet decisions usually make managements nervous. It is very important to have a systematic way to make such decisions.

MARKET TESTING

Products that pass the prototype development step must then be exposed to ultimate customers in some reasonably realistic market environment. This is an intense learning time. By now the product has taken on many more dimensions that can all affect its final destiny. Packaging, name, price, margins, reliability, variety of items, distributor support, shipping cases, credit terms, advertising and/or sales materials and sales training are just a few of the dimensions that may be added to a new product by the time it finally reaches the market. They all contribute to its success, or failure. Thus, the "total offering" must be tested in the market to ensure that all dimensions are working together and in the way that you assumed they would. This is the fine-tuning step.

Decisions made at the market testing step are almost always balance sheet decisions because they ask the company to commit large sums of money over a short period of time to finance full market introduction. These decisions also have implications beyond the financial vice president. They reflect on the competence of the management of the company among customers, suppliers, employees and the broader financial community. These are the biggest decisions you have made since you made the decision to step up your new product development activity. It should be quite clear that a systematic approach to making such decisions is required.

ENTERING FULL COMMERCIALIZATION

When a new product passes the market testing and moves on to a full market expansion, a rather abrupt change takes place. Up to this point, the project has been relatively small involving few people in some limited area. To achieve full commercialization requires involving a great many people in a much larger area.

Unless this change in the character of the project is carefully planned for, debilitating surprises can occur, such as raw material shortages, unavailable packaging materials, products without orders or orders without products, poor sales support, missed advertising deadlines. Figure 4 is an example.

CHOOSING A "CHAMPION"

The one inviolate rule learned in the past two decades about new product development is that people are the most important ingredient. New product development requires different skills and motivations than are found in the rest of a company. Career paths are different. Work structure tends to be unstable and temporary rather than well-defined and relatively permanent as is the case in most other departments. The chief executive officer requires even greater management skills here than is true anywhere else in the company.

Except in the very smallest company, no new product will ever

---

PACKAGING PROBLEMS AT HUNT-WESSON

When Hunt-Wesson Foods, Inc., the Fullerton, California food products company, introduced its new Super Wesson shortening to the food service market, the product was designed to replace two older products. Packaging for the old products had been bought on a "Minimum-Maximum" basis. That is, the package supplier guarantees to always have a minimum amount of packaging on hand. But he also has the right to manufacture up to some maximum quantity so as to be able to economize on the length of the production runs.

Basically, the customer owns all of the packaging between the minimum and maximum quantities. As the packaging for the new product was being ordered, the Purchasing Department discovered that the packaging for both old products was at maximum quantities.

It was prohibitively expensive to rehabilitate the old packaging and it had virtually no scrap value. To destroy the old packaging and absorb the full costs would have delayed profitability on the new product by a full two years.

The final decision was to continue to ship the old products into the Southeast Region of the United States until the old packaging was used up, thus delaying the introduction of the new product into that region. In fact, this process took 18 months.

During this period, there were severe disruptions in sales training, advertising, warehousing and customer relations, to name only a few of the problem areas. The real cost of the decision, although probably incalculable, was probably more than destroying the packaging would have been. The point is that it was all avoidable with better planning.

Figure 4. A case of costly lack of planning

successfully get to market unless it has a "Champion." One person must accept the responsibility for guiding. pushing, cajoling and persuading the initial ill-defined idea all through the development process. But what happens to a champion when his product is successful and is being managed by someone else? Or, what happens if the product idea dies? These are just some of the very real people problems that occur in new product development.

REALITIES ABOUT NEW PRODUCT DEVELOPMENT

Several realities about new product development must be thoroughly understood and carefully planned before you attempt to establish the new product development process in your company, or substantially upgrade the one you have now.

If the implications of these realities about new product development are not fully appreciated and firmly accepted by the top management of your company, your efforts will fail regardless of how lucky or creative you are.

The reason is that all three realities relate directly to the financial condition of the company.

NEW PRODUCT DEVELOPMENT TAKES TIME

At Dun & Bradstreet (see Figure 6) it takes an average of 24 months for an idea to move to market testing. It takes another nine months in test market and another one to five years to full profit realization. That means that the shortest amount of elapsed time is around three years and the longest around eight years.

Consumer product manufacturers usually can't match those turnaround times. Industrial product manufacturers frequently require even longer development time periods.

In developing new products from radically new technology, the time horizons stretch even farther out in the distance.

Just one example: RCA, SONY, Magnavox and other companies are now attempting to build a market for video disc machines. At the rate the market is developing, they will be at it well into the 1980's. Yet all the technology upon which these products are built has been available since the 1930's. Working prototype models were shown to the trade and the press as long ago as 1972.

While you can't change the time problem, you can do three things to soften its impact.

1. Make certain that each key member of your top management group understands this reality. Discuss it with them. Determine what their specific reactions would be if they didn't see a single new product on the market for three years.

2. Make certain that you have *one* easy and quick product in the development process right away. Don't skip any of the phases of the development process. But do push it out as fast as possible.

   The most likely candidates are line extensions, or something close to your existing product line. That means it probably won't be a big winner in sales dollars.

   What it will do is shift the discussion of your company's new product activity from an absolute basis (we've got nothing to show for all that time and money) to a relative one (we've got something, we'd like more, however).

3. Implement the development process controls outlined in the rest of this manual as carefully as you can. This is your best insurance that good projects will move through the process as rapidly as possible and that bad projects will be discarded as soon as possible so they do not tie up development manpower and funds any longer than is absolutely necessary.

RECOGNIZING REAL PROFITABILITY

Money that you spend today on new product development comes *directly out of today's profits.* Further, since most of that money will be spent on salaries, there won't be much to show for it today. The corollary to that is that if you didn't spend money on new product development, today's profits would be greater.

Not only short-term profitability is affected by new product development. The nonprofit Boston-based Strategic Planning Institute is engaged in some of the most sophisticated research ever undertaken into the effects of R&D spending on longer term profitability. In examining the results of over two thousand businesses of all types, they found the following general relationships between profits (measured as average return on investment over a four-year period) and R&D spending (measured as average R&D dollars divided by average sales dollars over the same four-year period).

R&D/SALES RATIO	ROI
0% to 0.4%	23%
0.4% to 1.2%	27
1.2% to 2.2%	23
2.2% to 3.9%	20
3.9% and over	18

This is not quite the whole story, however. It frequently turns out that businesses that spend heavily on R&D have other characteristics that work to depress ROI. The best strategy is to find the most profitable level of R&D spending which is a "normal" level for your business and its characteristics. Thus, an R&D spending strategy is in order.

CREATING YOUR OWN R&D SPENDING STRATEGY

To develop the outlines of your R&D spending strategy, start with the box below. This shows the characteristics of "normal" spending levels at each end of the spending range.

Examine your business to determine how closely it fits either of these extremes. If it fits either extreme reasonably well, you have an indication of what generally is the most profitable R&D spending level. If your business is somewhere in between, your spending strategy should probably lie somewhere in between. To help you focus your strategy, Figure 5 shows the R&D spending as a percent of sales for a

Market Characteristic	Normal Level of R&D Spending	
	Low*	High**
Stage in PLC	Saturation	Expansion
Real market growth (in constant dollars)	Average	Above average
Vertical integration (ratio of value added to sales)	Low	Above average
Investment intensity	Below average	Above average
New product introductions	Average	High
Market share	Average	Above average
New product sales introduced in the past three years as a percent of total sales (relative to competitors)	Below average	High

*Low is defined as an average of 0.5% of sales or less
**High is defined as an average of 4.0% of sales or more

variety of U.S. industries for 1979. In addition, it shows the highest and lowest ratio for an individual company in the industry.

As a useful exercise in helping to develop your R&D strategy, look at all of the *industries* that meet the "normal" high spending level (4.0%+) and compare their *industry* characteristics with the *individual business* characteristics in the box above. Do the characteristics for high spending describe the industry? Now do the same thing for the industries that spend at the low "normal" level (0–5%). Do they fit? Now characterize in-between industries.

For instance, containers (0.8%), paper (0.8%), steel (0.6%) and tires (0.6%) are all just above the low "normal" spending mark. How do they differ from the low spending characteristics? How are they the same? Now make a group next to the high spending level and ask the same questions. Work your way to the middle of the range. Where does your industry fit in the grid you have constructed? Where does your company fit?

R & D SPENDING LEVELS

INDUSTRY	R & D/SALES	HIGH	LOW
Aerospace	4.2%	6.5%	1.2%
Appliances	1.5	4.5	0.7
Automotive	3.2	4.0	0.7
Auto parts, equipment	1.5	2.5	0.8
Building materials	1.1	4.1	0.4
Chemicals	2.3	6.6	0.3
Conglomerates	1.6	3.0	0.2
Containers	0.8	1.2	0.2
Drugs	4.8	8.9	1.3
Electrical	2.8	8.9	0.6
Electronics	2.5	8.9	0.9
Food and beverages	0.5	2.9	0.1
Petroleum	0.4	1.2	0.1
Computers and peripherals	6.1	14.0	1.5
Office equipment	4.2	5.4	0.7
Instruments	3.9	11.2	0.7
Recreation products	4.2	8.0	0.5
Farm and construction equipment	2.7	3.8	0.7
Machine tools	1.6	8.6	0.5
Mining and metals	0.5	2.1	0.2
Oil supply and service	1.7	3.7	0.6
Paper	0.8	3.2	0.2
Personal care products	1.7	6.1	0.4
Semiconductors	5.7	10.1	1.3
Steel	0.6	2.6	0.4
Telecommunications	1.0	6.1	3.0
Textiles and apparel	0.6	3.0	0.2
Tires and rubber	1.7	2.5	0.5

Figure 5. Research and development average spending levels

As you do this exercise, remember that the box on the previous page is describing individual businesses, while the R&D spending levels are describing entire industries. The differences between the high and low spending rates within an industry point out the considerable differences that occur *within* that industry.

MORE ON R&D SPENDING STRATEGIES

New product development requires funds beyond R&D expenditures, frequently substantial sums. Total new product expenses for companies and for industries are simply not obtainable. But fairly accurate R&D numbers are available. Since new product expenses are generally proportionate to R&D numbers, the former can serve as a reasonable basis for planning.

The previous discussion was directed toward finding a normal spending strategy for your business that fits its characteristics. That generally appears to be the most profitable strategy. But it is by no means your only alternative.

You could select a very aggressive strategy and make it pay off handsomely. 3M (Minnesota Mining & Manufacturing) has a corporate goal that every division's sales must have 25% from products that did not exist five years ago. To support this goal, they spend heavily in R&D some two to three times the average. And it certainly pays off for them.

On the other hand, you might select an absolute minimum spending strategy. To do this you would install a very sensitive information system to inform you very quickly of competitors' new product entries. You would quickly evaluate them and attempt to duplicate the ones that you judge have real market potential. Be aware that such a strategy won't make you very popular at industry conventions and that your lawyers might get more telephone calls than they usually do, but it is an alternative you might consider.

WHY NEW PRODUCTS FAIL

How do you strike a position between zero risk, where all opportunities are lost, and risks that are so large that the company's balance sheet is in danger?

An examination of the reasons that new products fail is quite useful in understanding what risks are involved. Studies of why new products fail have produced a surprising amount of consistency in their findings.

One famous study examined a wide range of consumer and

industrial new products that had failed in the market and attempted to identify the reasons for failure. The results were:

Inadequate market analysis	32%
Product defects	23
Higher costs than anticipated	14
Inadequate marketing effort	13
Poor timing	10
Competitive reaction	8
	100%

Sourc ?

A more recent study of several hundred *industrial* new product failures produced these results:

The market was not big enough (inadequate market analysis)	28%
Me-too products	24
Technical failures	15
Prices were too high	13
Competitive reaction	13
No customer need for product	7
	100%

The most recent study examined 24 very large consumer packaged goods manufacturers. The companies chosen for study were selected because they had demonstrated outstanding growth all through the 1970's.

The researchers studied both the successes and the failures of these generally successful companies. They identified a dozen factors presumed to affect new product success and found that the factors fell into one of three groups: 1) Play little or no role in success, 2) Crucial to success, and 3) Not critical, but may contribute to the degree of success or failure. The groups and factors are:

Group 1: Little or no role
The product category or market
Packaging
Competitive reaction

Group 2: Crucial to success
   A real consumer need exists
   The product concept offers meaningful benefit
   The product actually delivers the benefit
   The advertising can communicate the benefit

Group 3: Not critical
   Product name
   Pricing
   Advertising spending level
   Promotion level and type
   Familiarity with technology
   Familiarity with channels of distribution

Management cannot control two aspects of the new product development process 1) technology and 2) competitive reaction. The finding that runs through all of this research is that *technical product failure* plays only a minor role in the overall picture and that competitive reaction plays an even smaller role. The great majority of new products fail because they were badly managed *inside* the company. That is something management can control.

When you view the risk in new product development from this perspective, it becomes clear that most—but not all—of the risk is in managing the process.

The difference between companies having long records of successes and those with strings of failures now becomes clearer. The difference is not likely to be luck, nor is it likely to be scientific genius. The difference is good management.

NOTING DIFFERENCES IN SIZE AND INDUSTRY

There are frequently signficant differences between consumer and industrial products in their physical characteristics, markets, buying processes, etc. This raises the question of whether there should also be different new product development processes.

The answer is "No." The process is exactly the same. The differences come in the details of the execution at each stage in the process. Ways must be found to execute each stage that accurately reflect the objective of the stage.

Every technique described in this manual is being used right now by some large company somewhere in the world. Some of these techniques cost a lot of money. Does that mean that smaller companies can't use the new product development process?

Again, the answer is "No." In fact, it is *much* more important for smaller firms to use the process because the impact of a failure will be so much greater than on a large company.

Small firms must adapt the big company techniques so that they fit, are affordable and accomplish the objective at each stage.

They must also use being small to advantage. Two ways that a small company can almost always beat a big company are in staying close to customers and making fast decisions.

Figures 6 and 7 offer a vivid comparison of how two companies put their new product development processes into effect.

HOW ONE COMPANY PUTS THE PROCESS TO WORK

Dun & Bradstreet, Inc. is a New York-headquartered financial services firm. D&B, as it is frequently called, is best known for its credit reporting activities. D&B believes that if it is to maintain consistent internal growth, it must develop a steady stream of successful new products.

In order to do so, the company has adapted the new product development process to suit its own requirements. Since D&B's "products" are financial services, this is a good illustration of the fact that *product* is used in this manual to mean either product or service.

Guidelines for New Product Concepts

Top management at D&B has established 12 criteria for directing the search for new product concepts. They are:

1. The concept must fit the overall corporate image comfortably.
2. The finished product must be standardized.
3. The total sales and profit potential must be significant.

Figure 6. Dun & Bradstreet's methodical new product process

4. The customers must have a functional and repetitive need for the product.

5. The product requires management skills that already exist in-house, or can be developed in-house.

6. The concept offers the customer a unique, distinctive benefit.

7. The final product can be developed into a large business quickly and has a short payback period.

8. The new business has no known legal, social or governmental restrictions or limitations.

9. The new product must not require heavy development expenses.

10. The final product should not require much after-sales servicing.

11. The product can be based, at least in part, on existing production capacity.

12. The product is sold by a sales force.

Generating New Product Concept Ideas

D&B relies heavily on its own employees to generate new product ideas. Every employee—from credit reporters on the street to top management—is encouraged to submit ideas for consideration.

To encourage and support this activity, D&B has instituted a financial incentive program. Any employee who submits an idea that reaches national distribution receives a $5,000 bonus award. D&B is currently generating about seventy-five new product ideas a year. The majority of the ideas are submitted by the field sales force. Over the past few years, D&B has been introducing an average of three new products a year and most recent years have produced a 100% success rate.

Screening New Product Concepts

Ideas that are submitted are first screened by a top management committee chaired by the CEO. Members of the committee represent all major departments of the company. Each idea is "fleshed out" some-

Figure 6. Continued

what by new product development personnel before it is evaluated by the committee. The committee then analyzes each concept in terms of how well it meets the guidelines.

Those concepts that pass the committee are submitted to a second stage of screening. For this second stage, several mock-ups are made of the product. A limited number of interviews are conducted with potential customers.

The purpose of this research is to explore whether or not a pattern of need for the product actually exists, and to identify users who might help D&B with further product design. The results of this research are summarized in written form and sent back to the committee for review.

Here the project either moves forward to the next stage or is dropped. The committee gives primary attention to size of the potential sales, amount of profit potential and competition.

Prototype Development
Roughly one out of eight original ideas reaches second stage screening and about half of those pass on to prototype development. Prototype development at D&B begins with refining and re-refining the mock-up. A few potential customers are involved in this design work to ensure that the project stays on target. Variations are also developed and tested. At this point, the concept may go through three or four cycles of development and testing.

When a satisfactory model has been designed, limited production capacity is established, either in-house or through an outside supplier. The sales force then selects a limited number of potential customers to aid in further testing and refinement. The number is usually less than a dozen.

These potential customers are given the new product samples free of charge in return for a promise to provide detailed information about how well the new product fills their needs. This activity provides D&B with valuable information about possible production problems, pricing levels, repeat usage and comparisons with competition, as well as product performance data.

Figure 6. Continued

Business Analysis

When the project manager decides that new product design is right, a formal business plan is written. It includes at least:

- Sales strategy
- Product delivery strategy
- Advertising and promotion strategy
- Pricing strategy
- Staffing and organization strategy
- Test marketing strategy
- Controls and contingency plans
- Forecasts of revenue, profit, return on investment (ROI) and return on sales (ROS) for at least two years.
- Additional information on market trends, competition, business cycles' effects, personnel considerations and any social or legal implications.

At the same time that the business plan is being prepared, a production plan is prepared. Since data processing is key to most of D&B's services, very careful attention is given to the production plan to ensure that production capability will be available and that costs are fully understood. Production requirements for test marketing and full national introduction are included.

Finally, budgets are prepared to identify test market costs and national introduction costs.

The business plan, the production plan and the budgets are submitted to the committee for review and funding.

Market Testing

Projects that are approved and funded by the committee are then placed in test markets. This testing takes D&B at least three months and may last for over a year. They use the test market stage as an intensive learning period to determine how the complete program works in an actual market place environment.

Figure 6. Continued

The development group works closely with customers throughout the market test phase to ensure that accurate evaluations are being made and to determine just which program modifications are required.

Full Commercialization

When D&B decides that it has all the elements of the new product program correct, it begins to expand the program nationally following the revised business and production plans. This process may take a year or two if the new product is sold by the existing D&B sales force. If a new sales force is required, along with the appropriate support organization, this process may take up to five years.

Organization

D&B has been very careful to recognize the importance of people in new product development at every step of the process.

To begin, ideas are submitted directly to the CEO, who passes them to the Director of Product Planning. The Director of Product Planning reports to a Senior Vice President who in turn reports to the Chairman of the Board of Directors.

This gives new product development high visibility at D&B and provides hard evidence to D&B employees that new product development has the complete backing of top management.

At the market test step, D&B forms a venture group to manage the project. The venture group consists of three or four carefully selected people who will have the responsibility to guide the project into the test markets and ultimately into national distribution.

This venture group includes individuals who are good analyzers *and* individuals who are good at getting things done. This reduces the likelihood of either analyzing a project too much or the danger of rushing headlong into the market without careful evaluation.

The venture group is headed by a successful line manager who is rotated through new product development as a further part of his own career development process.

Figure 6. Continued

A Case of New Product Process Failure

Hunt-Wesson Foods, Inc. is a large food products company headquartered in Fullerton, California. The company was created by a merger of the Hunt Bros. Canning Company, a full line tomato canner, and the Wesson Oil Co., a processor of salad and cooking oil. Brands from both companies dominated their respective product categories.

In 1966, a new president was hired. He was worried that the company would not be able to grow much with its existing product lines because both already had such large shares of their markets. He decided that future growth would have to come from new products. So he hired a vice president and created a New Product Development Department.

He then set ROI criteria for evaluating new product proposals. Three different criteria reflected the differences in the company's technological strengths. R&D personnel convinced him that they knew everything there was to know about tomatoes. So he set the lowest ROI criteria for tomato-based new products. Because the plant and equipment for processing soybean and cottonseed oils into salad and cooking oil was fairly old, he set a somewhat higher ROI criteria for new products based on this technology. Finally, he set the highest ROI criteria for new products based on other technology.

Finding New Products

The new vice president understood that he and his new department represented a sizable piece of overhead. He decided that he had better show some results fast, so he focused his efforts on the tomato-based new product area as the one that held the most promise.

He literally toured Southern California supermarkets examining the tomato products sections looking for something to make that the company did not already make. But it seemed that the Hunt Brothers had already done about everything possible with tomatoes. He found a Hunt label in every category.

In a completely different part of the store, the pasta section, he found what he was looking for. It had large displays of Chef Boyardee spaghetti sauce. Here was a tomato-based new product opportunity! A marketing manager was assigned to draw up plans to enter the market,

Figure 7. A problem in the new product process at Hunt-Wesson

and an R&D group was assigned to develop a product equal to, and hopefully better than, Chef Boyardee. Everyone assigned to the project set about their jobs with great enthusiasm.

After three or four months of development work, H-W's Eastern Region Sales Manager, who was based in New York, heard about the project. He wrote to his boss, the sales vice president, and suggested that the real target should be a brand of spaghetti that was sold in his area called Ragu.

The two vice presidents talked about this for some weeks, but they couldn't decide what to do. The marketing manager suggested that they buy some "back" store audit data on the product category from A. C. Nielsen, the international research firm. That made everyone feel good so they agreed to do that.

Studying the Data

Analysis of the Nielsen data showed that 85 percent of the total market for spaghetti sauce was in the Northeast quadrant of the U.S., and that Ragu had an 80 percent share of that section. The remaining 15 percent of the total market was spread throughout the rest of the U.S. Chef Boyardee had about a 50 percent share of that market.

For the marketing manager, this new data was both good news and bad news. The bad news was that Ragu's formulation was markedly different from Chef Boyardee's, and the product development had to start all over. The better news was that the total market was much bigger than anyone had suspected, and it was all concentrated in a tight geographic area. The size of the market and the lower ROI requirements combined to provide a lot of potential advertising dollars.

As a result, the planning began to shift. The idea now was to reach product parity with Ragu and spend $5 million in advertising to buy a place on the grocery store shelf. The product development project in R&D, however, was not going quite as well as expected. When the R&D group finally decided that they had a formulation that beat Ragu, another six months had elapsed. The marketing manager didn't think the new formulation was as good as Ragu. He was beginning to think that R&D had oversold its technological capability with tomato products.

Figure 7. Continued

Testing New Products

In order to settle this disagreement, a major portion of the marketing research budget for this project was allocated to an extensive in-home test among consumers. It was to be a triangle test with Ragu, Chef Boyardee and the new Hunt product.

Because the whole project was now falling well behind schedule, there was considerable pressure to hurry the market research. In the midst of all of this time pressure, the young market research analyst assigned to proof-read the questionnaires failed to notice that the typist had left out the place on the questionnaire where the "blind" product sample tested by the consumer was to be recorded. There were no labels or other identification on the samples other than the code letter which was supposed to be recorded on the questionnaire.

Nobody noticed the omission until the questionnaires were returned for coding and tabulation. In an attempt to salvage something from the study, several members of the marketing research group read the lengthy questionnaires to search for clues to the text products' identities. The effort was partially successful. The researchers were able to place a large majority of the questionnaires into three groups because of similarity of comments. But they couldn't tell which product fit which group. And that became a big problem because one of the products was much better liked by the consumers who took part in the test than the other two.

The new product development people then read the questionnaires. They basically agreed with the research department's groupings. Then R&D personnel took the questionnaires and read them. They also agreed to the general grouping of the questionnaires. The disagreement came over which product was the better liked one. R&D thought the clues indicated that it was the Hunt product. New product development people thought that the same clues indicated that it was Ragu.

Trying to Solve Matters

Since the great majority of the marketing research budget had been spent, the test could not be re-done. Instead, a very small sample study was conducted in an attempt to get some insights. The results were that Ragu was preferred over the Hunt formulation. But the details were dif-

Figure 7. Continued

ferent from the consumer reactions in the original large sample study. Thus, no real conclusions were reached.

The marketing manager, however, felt that he had sufficient evidence to request a new formulation from R&D. He received it grudgingly. This started a sequence of smaller and smaller sample size tests of formulation after formulation. The Hunt products lost to Ragu each time although the differences were frequently difficult to interpret.

As the original budget plan had assumed at least parity with Ragu, each time a Hunt formulation lost one of these mini-tests, the budget was reduced. When the top management finally ran out of patience and ordered the introduction of Hunt's Suprema Spaghetti Sauce, the budget was $750,000.

Changing the Concept

As the R&D difficulties went on prior to introduction, a subtle shift from the original concept of why the product would succeed was taking place in the new product development group. Originally, the consumer benefit was to be "better than" other sauces. Then it became "as good as." As the lack of confidence grew that R&D could produce either of those, the emphasis shifted to the package and advertising as the reasons the product would succeed.

For example, a glass bottle was developed that was square on the bottom and round on the top. The uniqueness of this package was supposed to give the product maximum shelf impact, be visually exciting, convenient to use, etc. The product was no longer the benefit, it became the packaging, or the advertising. When the product was introduced, not only did it not sell, the unique package had a structural weakness called a "water hammer." When the package received a sharp jolt, the bottom broke off. When rail car loads of the product reached the East coast from the West coast where it was made, it had recieved quite a few jolts. Shipments were quite often not so much unloaded as cleaned up.

Compounding the Failure

After about five years had gone by and memories of the original problems began to dim, the project was revived. Remember, it was and is a big market. This time the concept was to develop a bland-tasting base

Figure 7. Continued

product and place a small packet of seasonings into a recess in a newly designed glass bottle package. Now the claim didn't have to be "better than," it could be "make your own."

This time the product only got to the test market stage. The problem turned out to be that the tape to hold the seasoning packet in place had to be so strong to avoid pilferage and general loss, that consumers had great difficulty in removing it. Further, those who did get the seasoning packet off didn't much care for the product they made with it. This one died too.

Still Another Attempt
After another five years had passed and all the veterans of the first and second introductions were no longer with the company, a new generation of product developer re-discovered the spaghetti sauce market.

These new executives were determined to have a real difference between their product and Ragu this time. In order to ensure this, they commissioned a flavor segmentation study. This study showed that there were several segments in the spaghetti sauce market in terms of the kinds of flavor they preferred. One of those segments really didn't like *any* of the flavors of the available products.

Using these findings for guidance, a new formulation was developed that the "orphan" segment really preferred. Given the confidence that this strong position generated, the "new" new product development group devised a sophisticated four-city market test designed to evaluate two different spending levels and two different copy treatments.

While Hunt's Prima Salsa Spaghetti Sauce has not been the failure that the earlier versions were, neither has it been a resounding success. It currently holds an 8 percent to 9 percent share of market and hasn't shown much change recently. The reason is that consumers who make up the target segment of the market and really do prefer Hunt's very different formulation are light users of the product category. That is to say, they just don't buy much spaghetti sauce.

As you read through the remainder of this manual, try to decide how you would have done things differently at each step in this development project.

Figure 7. Continued

V

Creating Your Own Guidelines for Developing New Products

In the last Section, you were offered a chance to develop and market an atomic powered airplane. You turned down the offer because you said you were not in that business.

That was an instinctive, accurate and wise decision. It was accurate because only a very few companies in the world are in the business of building large aircraft. It was wise because the investment in technology to develop such a product is most likely beyond your means. And this instinctive reaction came because the offer immediately made you feel uncomfortable.

But it was also an easy decision. The very uniqueness of the proposition made it easy. Very few new product development decisions are this easy, because they are seldom as unique as an atomic airplane. The newsletter, *New Product Development* (P. O. Box 1309, Point Pleasant, New Jersey, U.S.A. 08742) estimates that over 6,000 new products were introduced into the United States alone in 1981. Some of those new products were ones that might have interested you. But which ones? That is the hard question to answer.

ESTABLISHING GUIDELINES FOR YOUR COMPANY

The new product development process helps you establish guidelines for the kinds of new products that might interest you. These guidelines provide a focus for your search for new product ideas and a screen for evaluating new product ideas as they are proposed.

Guidelines serve an even more important function than merely as developmental tools. They establish what kind of a company you are going to have for the future.

Guidelines will focus your search functions and direct your developmental activities toward projects that meet your criteria. The guidelines define the kinds of products you will be selling in the future. These products in turn define your business in the future.

What is equally true, but less obvious, is that guidelines will also establish what products you *won't* develop. And, by extension, they define what businesses you won't be in. What you won't be doing can be as important as what you will be doing three, five, or even 10 years from now.

Guidelines actually provide a great deal of your company's strategy. That is why this part of the process is sometimes called developing "Product Strategy."

DEVELOPING PRODUCT STRATEGY

Experienced executives recognize that product strategy is closely related to strategic planning. Strategic planning, in its simplest form, asks three questions for the entire organization:

- Where are we now?
- Where do we want to go?
- How do we get there?

Strategic planning deals with existing products and markets, products and markets you might move into through acquisitions, and products and markets you might develop with new products.

Product strategy deals only with the third element. It begins by asking the questions "Where are we now?" and "Where do we want to go?" and ends by providing the answer to "How do we get there?" If your company already has a strategic plan, or is deeply in the strategic planning process, you've probably already done much of the work in developing guidelines for your company. Your task then involves refining the goals set for new products in your strategic plans into specific "yes" or "no" criteria.

You begin developing a product strategy by carefully analyzing your own company to identify its strengths and weaknesses. Those things which you do well are your strengths. The things which you don't do well are your weaknesses. The reason that you must identify your strengths is that they will form the basis for developing guidelines.

The overwhelming evidence, both research and observational, indicates that companies are most likely to succeed when they deal from strength and most likely to fail when they don't.

The reason that you improve your chances for success by building on your strengths is quite straightforward. You are simply less likely to make mistakes when you are working in an area you know well.

There are many examples of companies, large and small, that failed to understand that simple fact, and subsequently paid dearly for the failure. One of the more publicized examples in the 1970's was the Stamford, Connecticut-based Singer Company.

There was no question that Singer needed new products. The world market for home sewing machines, which Singer dominated, has been shrinking for many years. But Singer chose a foreign field—business machines and telecommunications equipment. When the ill-fated program came to an end in 1976, it was accompanied by a $411 million write-off!

IDENTIFYING STRENGTHS AND WEAKNESSES

Product Planning Page 3 will help you identify your strengths and weaknesses. This planning tool shows characteristics common to many businesses and provides a format for rating yourself, compared to *your competitors.*

It doesn't show all of the characteristics that relate to your particular industry. So your first step is to examine the items shown in Planning Page 3 in Figure 8 and eliminate the ones that don't apply to your industry. Then think carefully about the business characteristics that are truly important to success in your industry. Add these items to the Product Planning Page.

Then write evaluation definitions that are appropriate for your industry. Use the following as an example.

A Rating: Best in the business. Really strong. Much more than we need now. Unquestioned leader.

B Rating: Better than most. Quite strong. Not a problem.

C Rating: About average. O. K. Equal to the industry.

D Rating: Needs improvement. Falling off. Worrisome. Deteriorating. Used to be a lot better.

E Rating: A real problem. Needs action now. Must be corrected. Big trouble!

Make enough copies of your individualized version of Product Planning Page 3 for the key executives in your organization. You want all departments to participate in this exercise. It might surprise you to see how your marketing activities look to your production people.

EXPLAINING THE IDENTIFICATION PROCESS

Write a memo to accompany the Product Planning Pages. Make three points in the memo. 1) This activity is important and requires serious thought. 2) Characteristics that cannot be solidly evaluated by the individual should be left blank. 3) The results will remain confidential. Include a deadline not greater than two weeks away and follow up immediately on those Product Planning Pages that are not back by the deadline.

Product Planning Page 3

Company Profile

Definition of
A Rating:_____

_____

Definition of
B Rating:_____

_____

Definition of
C Rating:_____

_____

Definition of
D Rating:_____

_____

Definition of
E Rating:_____

_____

Characteristic		Rating			
	A	B	C	D	E

Marketing Area

	A	B	C	D	E
Market shares					
Product quality	—	—	—	—	—
Extent of distribution	—	—	—	—	—
Quality of distribution	—	—	—	—	—
Size of sales force	—	—	—	—	—
Effectiveness of sales force	—	—	—	—	—
Level of sales training	—	—	—	—	—
Selling expense	—	—	—	—	—
Prices	—	—	—	—	—
Customer base	—	—	—	—	—
Advertising budgets	—	—	—	—	—
Advertising effectiveness	—	—	—	—	—
Market research data base	—	—	—	—	—
Warehousing and shipping	—	—	—	—	—
Distribution expense	—	—	—	—	—
Overall margins	—	—	—	—	—
Market growth	—	—	—	—	—

Figure 8. A form to identify company strengths and weaknesses

	A	B	C	D	E
——————————	—	—	—	—	—
——————————	—	—	—	—	—
——————————	—	—	—	—	—
——————————					

Production Area

	A	B	C	D	E
Plant capacity	—	—	—	—	—
Plant location (s)	—	—	—	—	—
Ability to expand plant (s)	—	—	—	—	—
Age of plant (s)	—	—	—	—	—
Age of equipment	—	—	—	—	—
Condition of equipment	—	—	—	—	—
Versatility of equipment	—	—	—	—	—
Availability of labor	—	—	—	—	—
Quality of labor	—	—	—	—	—
Availability of raw materials	—	—	—	—	—
Quality of raw materials	—	—	—	—	—
Manufacturing expenses	—	—	—	—	—
Inventory control	—	—	—	—	—
Production scheduling	—	—	—	—	—
Proportion of defects	—	—	—	—	—
Quality control	—	—	—	—	—
Union relations	—	—	—	—	—

——————————	—	—	—	—	—
——————————	—	—	—	—	—
——————————	—	—	—	—	—
——————————	—	—	—	—	—
——————————	—	—	—	—	—

Financial Area

	A	B	C	D	E
Cash flow	—	—	—	—	—
Profits	—	—	—	—	—
Dividend record	—	—	—	—	—
Available credit	—	—	—	—	—
Available capital sources	—	—	—	—	—
Plan to actual performance	—	—	—	—	—
Bad debts	—	—	—	—	—
Inventory turnover	—	—	—	—	—
Customer payment record	—	—	—	—	—
Assets	—	—	—	—	—
Liabilities	—	—	—	—	—
Long term debt	—	—	—	—	—
Return on investment	—	—	—	—	—
Shareholder equity	—	—	—	—	—

Figure 8. Continued

	A	B	C	D	E
Share price/earnings ratio	—	—	—	—	—
Sales per employee	—	—	—	—	—
Ownership	—	—	—	—	—
	—	—	—	—	—
	—	—	—	—	—
	—	—	—	—	—
	—	—	—	—	—
	—	—	—	—	—

Administrative Area

	A	B	C	D	E
Clerical skills	—	—	—	—	—
Office facilities	—	—	—	—	—
Office procedures	—	—	—	—	—
Administrative costs	—	—	—	—	—
Customer service	—	—	—	—	—
Clerical turnover	—	—	—	—	—
Administrative skills	—	—	—	—	—
Training costs	—	—	—	—	—
Office equipment	—	—	—	—	—
	—	—	—	—	—
	—	—	—	—	—
	—	—	—	—	—
	—	—	—	—	—
	—	—	—	—	—

Management Area

	A	B	C	D	E
Top management experience	—	—	—	—	—
Middle management depth	—	—	—	—	—
Middle management experience	—	—	—	—	—
Management turnover	—	—	—	—	—
Salaries	—	—	—	—	—
Easy communications	—	—	—	—	—
Accurate information	—	—	—	—	—
Ability to make decisions	—	—	—	—	—
Well-defined responsibilities	—	—	—	—	—
Planning ability	—	—	—	—	—
Ability to anticipate events	—	—	—	—	—
Ability to react quickly	—	—	—	—	—

Figure 8. Continued

	A	B	C	D	E
_____	___	___	___	___	___
_____	___	___	___	___	___
_____	___	___	___	___	___
_____	___	___	___	___	___

Technology Area

	A	B	C	D	E
Age of product technology	___	___	___	___	___
Scientific capability	___	___	___	___	___
Engineering capability	___	___	___	___	___
Product patents	___	___	___	___	___
Process patents	___	___	___	___	___
R & D management	___	___	___	___	___
R & D expenses	___	___	___	___	___
R & D project success record	___	___	___	___	___
_____	___	___	___	___	___
_____	___	___	___	___	___
_____	___	___	___	___	___
_____	___	___	___	___	___
_____	___	___	___	___	___

Other Area

	A	B	C	D	E
_____	___	___	___	___	___
_____	___	___	___	___	___
_____	___	___	___	___	___
_____	___	___	___	___	___
_____	___	___	___	___	___
	___	___	___	___	___

Figure 8. Continued

Add up the number of "A's", "B's", etc. for each score for each characteristic and write them on a blank copy of Product Planning Page 3. Make enough copies of this summary version for those executives who are the real decision-makers in your organization. Circulate the copies with an invitation to a meeting to analyze the results and attempt to understand the implications.

FOCUS OF REVIEW MEETING

There are several things that you want to accomplish at that meeting. First, you want to get a consensus judgment of the group members that the composite profile of your company does seem to be accurate. If there is disagreement about this, you have to find out why, and develop some way to deal with it directly.

The next thing to do is examine the "E" and "D" items. Try to identify the real problem and then deal with it in a specific way. Assign an individual to handle it, or form a study group to recommend solutions.

Now you can turn your attention to the real purpose of the meeting, identifying your strengths. Look at the "A" items. Write them on a black board, or large sheet of paper that everyone can see. Look for patterns and characteristics that tend to cluster together. For instance, high product quality, good quality control, low labor turnover, high wages, low selling expenses, etc.

Look at the "B" items that might also fit into these patterns of strength to see which ones might be up-graded to "A" items with a modest amount of effort and/or money. Make assignments to do so.

Now try to find verbal ways to describe the groupings of "A" and up-graded "B" items. These are your company's strengths. Your new product development guidelines will be built on these strengths.

VI

Further Refining Your Guidelines: What Business Are You Really In?

Now that you have a good idea what your company's strengths are, and have moved to correct any weaknesses, it is time to turn to the second important question in developing guidelines.

That is the deceptively simple question, "What business are you in?" When executives encounter this question seriously for the first time, the reaction usually is, "We make _____." This is an inadequate definition for planning and development in successful companies.

REAL COMPANIES DEFINING ACTIVITIES

Defining the business is one of the greatest skills in the art of management. When it is done accurately and carefully, it can have a dramatic impact on the company's operations and profits. Some examples will make this clearer.

The Paper Mate Co. is a wholly-owned division of the Gillette Company, Inc., a consumer products company headquartered in Boston, Massachusetts. For many years, Paper Mate simply manufactured and sold medium priced ball point pens to retailers. Competitors had actually defined Paper Mate for itself. Bic Pen Corp. moved in to control the low price end of the market with its inexpensive throwaway pens. A.T. Cross Co. and the Parker Pen Co. were in solid command of the premium priced end of the market.

In the mid-1970's, a new president took over the Paper Mate division. One of his first tasks was to attempt to define the business that Paper Mate was in. The first answers that he got from his staff were, predictably enough, that they were in the ball point pen business. However, as they continued to analyze and think about the question, a different answer began to emerge. The final definition of their business came to be "facilitating written communication." This new definition has had a dramatic impact on the direction of the company.

Paper Mate began development of a low priced pen aimed at the office supply market. To support this new market thrust, it acquired the Liquid Paper Corp., a maker of typewriter correction fluid and ribbons. To strengthen Liquid Paper, it began the development of a group of correctable typewriter ribbons. It developed a pen with erasable ink to penetrate the premium priced pen market. And recently it introduced a correction fluid for pen and ink errors.

All of this new product development and acquisition activity took five years and is still on-going. You can see the difference the new definition has made on the products the company makes.

In Easton, Pennsylvania, the Binney & Smith Co. used to be in the business of making wax crayons. Their green and yellow crayon boxes accompanied most American children to school for almost a half century. By the early 1970's, Binney & Smith began to understand the implications of a declining birth rate for its business. Combined with the sharp increase in the raw materials costs for its wax-based products, these forced Binney & Smith to re-define its business.

The company now says it is "in the business of providing assorted products that are fun to use and inspire creative self-expression." This new definition has lead to a stream of new products, six in 1981 and eleven in 1982. Drinking mugs, coloring books and ink marking pens are examples. Wide use has been made of licensing arrangements. It put it's Crayola brand on products such as tote bags.

B&S capitalized on the hit Broadway play "Annie" to introduce a line of Little Orphan Annie products. It has made acquisitions in the commercial art field in order to market paints and brushes. Today's re-defined Binney & Smith is quite a different company than the one that in 1970 was simply in the business of making crayons.

The Bostitch Division of the Providence, Rhode Island conglomerate, Textron, Inc., used to define its business as "stapling and stitching machines, staples and wire." Now Bostitch defines its business as "fastening." This re-definition has led to glue, tape, tacks, rivets, welds and almost all the other means by which items are held together.

The large French company, Lafarge Coppée, is another interesting example. Lafarge is one of the world's major cement producers, and it is moving to enter the emerging biotechnology field. It is taking this direction after defining its business as "industrial fermentation." Further, it is not attempting to develop new micro-organisms, but concentrating on developing processes for mass-producing the organisms themselves and their by-products. Such an emphasis reflects Lafarge's understanding of what its strengths are.

These few examples make two points: 1) How you define your business can make a major impact on the products you develop and market, and 2) Defining a business is a highly individual affair. How you define your business challenges your insight and creativity. While there are no strict rules for defining a business, two tools will help you with the task.

THE SERVED MARKET CONCEPT

The new business definitions illustrated above were different from the "old" definitions in that they included a combination of product (or process in the case of Lafarge) and customer, instead of just focusing on the products. A new business definition must account for customers. This seems simple, but in practice it can be very difficult. Even for the maker of a single product, defining the market offers many levels of choices.

Consider the choices facing a manufacturer of instant coffee located in the United Kingdom. Is the correct market:

- Decaffeinated instant vs. regular instant?
- All instant coffee in the U.K.?
- All coffee in the U.K.?
- All instant coffee in the European Common Market?
- Coffee sold in restaurants as well as in grocery stores?

There are no easy answers to those questions. But for most companies, the appropriate market is never the total market, it is some segment of the total market. This leads to examining parts or segments of the market.

Markets are made up of segments because differences exist among customers, among needs, among competitors. Similar customers with similar needs served by similar products are clustered together. They form market segments. Note that the key word is similar, not identical.

The served market concept attempts to define market segments which you dominate, where you are the strongest competitor. A served market is defined as that combination of customers and products/services with respect to which you alone have a competitive advantage over all others. This involves considering your total offering to the customer. It includes delivery, price, credit terms, warrantees, etc., as well as the product itself.

Each of your competitors has served markets where they maintain competitive advantages. Each served market also has a boundary line. That boundary is delineated by the point of zero competitive advantage. It is along these boundary lines that all competition takes place. This competition fundamentally assumes two forms. One is where you attempt to convince your competitors' customers that your offering actually has the better value.

The other form of competition takes place in developing new products that offer your competitors' customers better value than their offerings. This second form of competition is why the served market concept is of particular interest in developing product strategy. You can visualize the served market concept like the box below.

Product Planning Page 4 in Figure 9 enables you to try to define your own served markets.

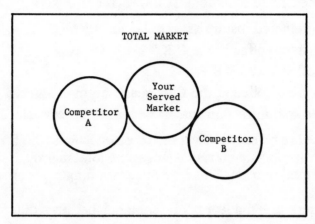

The Served Market Concept

ADDING A THIRD DIMENSION

Adding a second dimension—customers—to the definition of a business increases the depth of product strategy. You can take the definition of the business one step further and add a third dimension to examine market structures in three dimensional space.

By way of illustration, recall Paper Mate's definition of its business, "facilitating written communication." Implicit in that definition are two dimensions.

One is a certain group of customers, for example, business people, or housewives, or students, and a certain set of customer benefits, such as recording orders, or compiling a shopping list, or taking notes. Paper Mate examined each of these "intersections" of customer group and customer benefit to find unmet needs and, therefore, new product opportunities.

Product Planning Page 4

Defining Served Markets

Product A:
Definition
of Served
Market

Product B:
Definition
of Served
Market

Figure 9. A definition sheet for the served market concept

Product Planning Page 4

Defining Served Markets

Product C:
Definition
of Served
Market

Product D:
Definition
of Served
Market

Figure 9. Continued

The dimension that affects Paper Mate's business that is not included in its definition is the technology by which customer benefits are delivered to customer groups. Judging by Paper Mate's actions, it would seem that the firm limited its interest in technology to just two forms in which written communication can take place, i.e. pen and ink on paper, and typewriters on paper.

But certainly there are other technologies for delivering written communication. Some that exist right now are:

- Electronic typewriters
- Cable television channels that reproduce, say, share market reports
- Telex
- Microfilm and microfiche
- Satellite transmission of, say, sporting events' scores
- Letterpress, offset, rotogravure printing
- Carbon pencil
- Facsimile transmission
- Sky writing

The last one may be a little out of the ordinary, but it does help to make the point. When you begin to add the technology by which the customer benefit is delivered to the customer group, a whole new set of definitions becomes possible.

Also, each of these new three dimensional market segments can grow at different rates with varying degrees of attractiveness for new product development. Further, this sort of analysis may identify "empty" market segments where new products might profitably create new markets.

DIAGRAMMING THE THREE DIMENSIONAL CONCEPT

Figure 10 represents how airlines might visualize travellers to or from a particular destination. They could use it to visualize those travellers by origin, or by destination. As you can see, there is a significantly

Three Dimensional Travel Market Structure

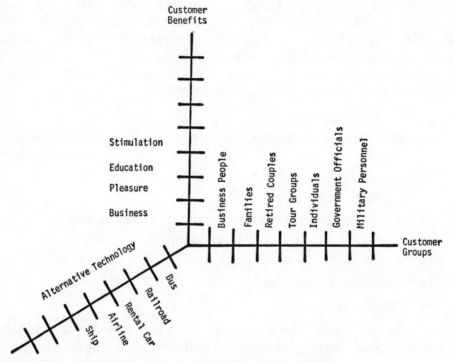

Figure 10. A three dimensional analysis structure for airlines

greater amount of analytical power in this three dimensional structure than in the more conventional two dimensional method.

Product Planning Page 5 in Figure 11 provides a place for you to experiment with developing three dimensional representations of your markets and your business. You will find it a demanding exercise. If your structures are incomplete, don't worry. It's a situation that you can keep returning to as new ideas and insights occur to you.

When you have completed Product Planning Page 5 for each product to your satisfaction, circulate them to your key group. After about a week, hold a meeting to discuss them and to come to agreement on at least a tentative working definition of your business.

Three Dimensional Market Structures

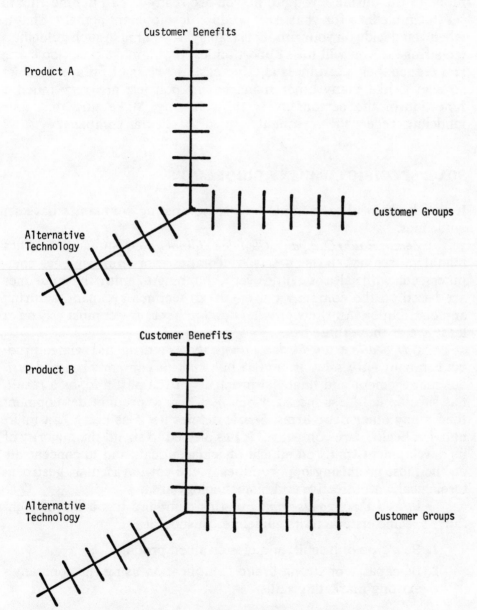

Figure 11. Form for three dimensional analysis of market structure

DECIDING ON NEW PRODUCT DEVELOPMENT GUIDELINES

When you have a clear picture of your strengths and a working definition of the business you are in, you are ready to call the meeting to
set the guidelines for your new product development activity. That is
when you decide on your product strategy. If you make such guidelines
too stringent, you will miss opportunities. If you make them too loose,
you reduce their usefulness and increase the risks of failure. Product
strategies, like many other management policies, are very much a
reflection of the personality of the company. Make sure that your
guidelines reflect the personality of your particular company.

SOME SPECIFIC COMPANY GUIDELINES

It may be helpful to examine how some existing companies have set
guidelines.

Zenith Radio Company, Glenview, Illinois; a consumer electronics
manufacturer of television sets, videotape recorders, personal computers, etc. with sales of a little over $1 billion. At Zenith, the guidelines
are based on the company's strengths in technology, manufacturing
and distribution. Any new product development project must rely on at
least two of these three bases.

G.D. Searle & Co., Skokie, Illinois; this is a drug and related product company with sales around $1 billion. This company has had seri-
ous management and financial problems in the past and, as a result,
has substantially less money available for new product development
than many other drug firms. Searle defines itself as being "an international health care company." It has elected to spend the majority of
its development funds on ethical pharmaceuticals and to concentrate
on the most promising opportunities in the cardiovascular, gastroen-
terological, anti-infective and biotechnology areas.

U. K. bakery goods company; this company has a list of eight
fairly specific criteria in its guidelines. It should:

1. Be a type of biscuit, or a closely allied product.
2. Be capable of strong brand identification using the company's
   existing marketing skills.

3. Be capable of formulation by the company's R&D department, using existing expertise.

4. Be capable of manufacture without excessive capital outlay.

5. Be suited to the company's existing marketing and sales organization.

6. Be consonant with the company's existing distribution facilities.

7. Be likely to be selling profitably in its second year and to break even, taking into account launch expenses, by the end of the third year.

8. Be considered to have adequate profit potential, i. e., annual sales, not less than £1 million. Manufacturer's profit margin, not less than 20 percent. Annual profit, after marketing and advertising, not less than 9 percent.

Figure 12 offers a complete set of guidelines developed by a California firm.

Knudsen Corporation, Los Angeles, California is a dairy and food products company with an extensive set of guidelines.

A. Business Considerations

There are four separate areas of business considerations that should be carried out for the evaluation of any new product under investigation:

. . . sales volume potential

. . . financial/profit potential

. . . product line compatability

. . . competitive strength evaluation

For each of the above areas of investigation, there are a series of questions to be answered relative to the new product. The cumulative results of the answers to each question—as well as the mea-

Figure 12. A complete set of guidelines at the Knudsen Corporation

surement of the sales potential and financial potential—provide an analytical base for a "go" or "no go" decision for the new product.

1. Sales Volume Potential

a. What is the current retail grocery sales volume of all competitive brands?

b. What other product categories are considered substitute buying options by the consumer, and how would these indirect competitive categories be affected?

c. What are the trends of sales growth of these direct and indirect product categories?

d. What share-of-market could a Knudsen product entry reasonably expect to capture (consider both direct and indirect competitive brands)?

e. (If product is an acquisition) What is current market sales volume and what additional sales volume could Knudsen reasonably expect to add through its marketing capabilities?

f. Is the projected sales volume sufficient to warrant gaining and holding distribution in the grocery store?

2. Financial/Profit Potential

a. What capital investments are necessary for attainment of production at the projected sales volume?

b. Is cost of raw materials stable and available? Are there any shortage forecasts that might cause higher prices and/or shortages of raw materials for either product or packaging needs?

c. What marketing investments must be made in sales, distribution, advertising and merchandising to:
... support first year of product introduction;
... achieve brand share and sales volume projections; and
... maintain projected product sales after introductory period?

d. At what sales level is a break-even point achieved? Is this break-even point significantly below projected sales volume?

Figure 12. Continued

e. When selling at a competitive retail price, and allowing for retail and trade margins, will the product generate a gross profit margin equal to or in excess of current products?

f. Does the return on investment projection for the product being considered offer the best alternative use of capital:
   . . . compared to other new product considerations?
   . . . compared to further investment in current product line?

g. What is the projected payout or break-even point on capital investment and introductory marketing investment in terms of months after product introduction date?

3. Product Line Compatibility

a. Is this product liable to take sales from any current Knudsen products? If so, will the resultant sales of both products be larger in total sales volume or share-of-market?

b. Does this new product have a seasonal sales pattern or economic cycle of sales potential that is complementary to current Knudsen products?

c. Is grocery store distribution of this product compatible with sales call efficiency of Knudsen sales force (Sold in the same sections of the store and sales through the same chain buyer as other Knudsen products)?

d. Is this product to be purchased by the same consumer who buys other Knudsen products and is familiar with the Knudsen brand and quality?

e. (If product is perishable) Is there sufficient shelf life of product to satisfy projected grocery store turnover rates?

f. (If product is to be manufactured within current Knudsen plant) Is product equipment, raw material, warehousing of finished goods, and packaging compatible with current Knudsen products to allow additional use of present investment in plant facilities and equipment?

Figure 12. Continued.

4. Competitive Strength Evaluation

a. What competitive advantages does the potential product have over competitive brands?

b. Is the competitive product advantage one that can be maintained by patent, copyright, formulation or production advantages?

c. What government regulation or legislative acts can possibly eliminate a product advantage or a restriction on the product category?

d. Do major grocery chains currently have private label entries that might restrict distribution or cause a price squeeze of branded products?

e. What are recent changes in brand shares of direct and indirect competitive products that might indicate a competitive weakness?

f. What is current stage of the product life cycle? Are there many brands fighting for position on a product development, or are there a few major, entrenched brands in a mature or declining product life cycle stage?

B. Unsatisfied Consumer Needs

The second major area of investigation in the new product evaluation analysis is to determine the unsatisfied consumer needs underlying the product usage situation. While this evaluation is most important in the initial screening of any new product consideration, it is also valuable in the new product development and the strategic positioning of the product.

By determining that there are unsatisfied consumers needs that are not being met by existing competitive products and identifying these needs, Knudsen can ascertain:

. . . that there is an existing product weakness to be exploited;

. . . that there is a market need for an additional product; or

. . . that a Knudsen product entry in this category must generate sales by obtaining a market share among existing customers and among existing brands.

Figure 12. Continued

The areas of investigation to determine the unsatisfied consumer needs are as follows.

. . . What are the basic needs underlying the product usage situation?

. . . What are the basic motivations underlying the brand purchase decision? physical needs? psychological needs?

. . . How important are each of these needs?

. . . To what extent are these needs being satisfied by the existing products?

C. Product Differentiation

The third major area of investigation in the new product analysis is a product differentiation analysis. This is a comparative analysis to determine where and how the new product being considered can best gain a competitive advantage in fulfilling an unsatisfied need.

Two separate areas of comparison should be made:

. . . Does the new product entry offer competitive *physical* product differences that are perceivable?; that are important to the consumer?

. . . Does the new product entry offer competitive *image* product differences that differentiate this product from competition? that are important to the consumer?

Another viewpoint of analysis of product differentiation is through the evaluation of the following questions:

a. Does the product fulfill a consumer need better than a competitive brand, an advantage in form, convenience, taste, nutrition, new uses, etc.?

b. Is the competitive advantage one that is apparent to the consumer and/or can the advantage be communicated through advertising?

Figure 12. Continued.

c. Is the consumer need and product advantage applicable to all consumers of the product, or to only a segment of potential users? Is this segment broad enough to support the projected sales volume?

d. Does the product offer an advantage of price and/or value to consumer commensurate with the value of the product differentiation?

e. What social changes (environmental, family composition, family income, nutritional/dietary trends) are evident or forecast that might affect the product differentiation based on changing consumer needs?

Figure 12. Continued

VII

Generating Ideas
for New Product Concepts

Where does a good idea come from? The answer is "anywhere!" And when can a good idea come along? That answer is "anytime!" However, if you simply sit back and wait for the inspiration method of generating ideas for new product concepts, you probably won't be very happy with the results. It's not that some pretty terrific ideas haven't happened that way. It's just that if you use that method, you lose control of the process.

YOU NEED NUMEROUS IDEAS

The new product development process requires a lot of new ideas and an on-going flow of new ideas. The inspiration system fails on both counts. In fact, the one step in the process that is most often mismanaged is generating enough new ideas.

A company may start with five or six ideas, lose a couple of them to screening, another in business analysis. Then another one doesn't make it through prototype development. Suddenly the new product development people are feeling a lot of pressure to show some results. Soon, the only product left is going to test market. And the odds are good that it will fail.

Research has shown that, on the average, it takes 58 initial ideas to get *one* commercially successful new product to market. It is easy to see why the odds are against success when you start with only a few ideas.

This Section outlines a variety of ways in which companies generate lots of ideas for new product concepts. There is no single method that is best for you. You will likely use a combination of methods that best suit your industry, your people and your technology. There will be a lot of trial and error along the way to develop the process that works best for you.

ENCOURAGING CREATIVITY

The entire new product development process requires creativity, but generating new ideas is pure creativity. It's a good idea to look at what experts know about creativity. Because it is so obvious that creativity is so very valuable, hundreds and hundreds of studies have been conducted and countless dollars have been spent over the past two decades trying to understand what creativity is, who has it and how it can be nurtured. There's not much to show for all that effort.

There are creative people and uncreative people. The uncreative people wonder where in the world the creative people get all those ideas. The creative people wonder why everybody cannot see the same things they see. There is a lot more creativity around than most people suspect.

The creative process involves combining two previously dissimilar ideas in a new way that "creates" a new idea. It's finding a pattern among elements that didn't seem to have a pattern before.

EXAMPLES OF CREATIVE THINKING

Federal Express, Inc., the Memphis, Tennessee air package carrier, is one of the outstanding success stories of the 1970's. Federal Express went from zero to $1 billion in sales in less than nine years by providing overnight delivery of small packages between any major U.S. cities.

Packages are gathered every afternoon all over the U.S. and flown to Memphis. There they are sorted and re-routed to their destinations. Thus, a package going from New York to Philadelphia, a hundred miles apart, will travel over a thousand miles to reach its destination. Fred W. Smith, the founder of Federal Express, got the idea while thinking about how central banking systems clear their financial instruments each day.

Harold Leventhal wanted to send a lawyer in Washington, D.C. a present to show his appreciation over a large case that had just been won. Flowers or candy didn't seem to quite fit the occasion. A magnum of Dom Perignon champagne was better suited.

When he tried to send the champagne, he found that it was illegal to ship wine across state lines. It occurred to him that the Florist Telegraph Delivery service (FTD) "shipped" flowers all over the U.S. without ever crossing state lines. He acquired a partner, a small amount of start-up capital, a toll-free telephone number and set out to sign up liquor stores in major cities. Four years later, Leventhal's privately owned Tele-wine Company has a system of 9,000 cooperating liquor stores, a growing corporate client list, and profits.

All during the 1960's, Milt Kuolt worked for the Boeing Company in Seattle, Washington. On weekends, he and his family liked to take trips camping in their trailer. He found that public campgrounds were often run-down, noisy and without activities for his children. He considered developing a small rural piece of land that he owned into a campground and selling off individual campsites. That way he would get the kind of place he wanted.

The problem with that idea was that there would be no revenues for upkeep. Just about that time he heard about the first time-share resort projects that were being built. The joint ownership was just the key concept that he needed, but with a variation. Kuolt developed a series of campgrounds and sold lifetime memberships that were good at any of his campgrounds. A modest annual membership fee from all the members covers upkeep. It took 12 years, but by 1980, Kuolt's Thousand Trails, Inc. had 14 campgrounds, 25,000 members, sales of $34 million and earnings of $4.5 million.

In 1980, Houston, Texas financier Charles E. Hurwitz found that he had a lot of his assets in illiquid real estate. It occurred to him that there might be a lot of other people who were locked into their holdings because of poor market conditions, high interest rates or tax considerations. He had heard of a way that successful oil well speculators recover their investments by creating a company and issuing stock backed by the well's proven reserves.

To make that idea fit his problem, Hurwitz formed MCO Equities, Inc., backed by his own holdings. He began to trade MCO stock for commercial, industrial or multi-family residential properties worth at least $2.5 million each. The investor trades his assets for a stake in a diversified real estate pool.

When MCO Equities went public on the American Stock Exchange in 1982, the company held assets in excess of $1 billion. That makes it one of the largest real estate empires in the U.S.

In each of these cases, an individual took two separate concepts, ideas, or patterns, and re-combined them to create a new entity. That's creativity at work.

One last point about creativity. Creativity alone is never enough. There was a lot of very hard work put into each of those four businesses. Thomas Edison used to like to say that invention was "1% inspiration and 99% perspiration."

SOURCES FOR GENERATING NEW IDEAS

A simple, straightforward, convenient source of new product concepts can be found among *your own employees*. They know a lot about your company, your products and your customers. The best of them think a lot about how to do their jobs better, and that can include ideas for new products. The objective is to show them that you are serious about it and to provide a means for them to submit ideas. A suggestion box on the wall is not sufficient.

At Dun & Bradstreet, you'll recall, ideas are submitted directly to the President. That certainly gives new ideas importance in the company. The $5,000 bonus for successful products makes it worthwhile to think about new products.

It is doubtful that any company in the world has done a better job of creating a new products "culture" among its employees than

Minnesota Mining and Manufacturing (3M). Year after year, 20% to 25% of its sales come from products introduced within the past five years. Every time a new product reaches $1 million in profitable sales (remember, this is a $5 billion sales company), the entire development team is singled out for attention and honored. Everyone in the company knows that if he or she can invent a new product, or develop one that others have abandoned, that person will have a chance to manage the product as if it were their own.

Ideas are solicited continually and tested quickly when they are submitted. Ideas are *never* killed without testing them. As soon as an idea passes initial testing, 3M assembles a development team from technology, marketing, production and finance. The team stays together from inception to national introduction. Rewards are passed out as each step is successfully accomplished. In case a product fails, the people are re-assigned, never fired.

3M has its own version of the Nobel Prize, called the Carlton Award after an early president of the company. It is awarded each year to a few scientists who have made major contributions over the course of their careers at 3M. There have only been 20 awards in 18 years and the award winners have a very special status in the company.

3M has a collection of "folklore" that keeps getting repeated. Here is an example. One 3M employee persisted in trying to find a way to use reject sandpaper minerals. At one point, he was actually fired because of the time and effort he spent on the problem. Still, he just kept on coming to work.

His solution to the problem led to 3M's Roofing Granules Division. When the obstinate employee finally did leave 3M, he retired as Vice President of the division. 3M makes a real effort to keep such stories alive to motivate current employees.

ANOTHER INTERNAL SOURCE

Your sales people are also your employees, but they occupy such a position that they deserve special treatment as a source of new product ideas. The sales people are the ones who are in constant contact with your customers and are in the best position to spot unmet customer needs.

In industrial markets, it is particularly important that you encourage sales people to observe their customer's operations and to report back suggestions for new products. The reason is straightforward. Industrial products companies have fewer customers than consumer products companies, so each individual customer is much more important.

McCormick & Co. is a large spice and flavoring company headquartered in Hunt Valley, Maryland. McCormick has a sales force of over 600 people and makes use of an interesting device which it calls the Sales Board. There are 20 members on the Sales Board, all of whom are also members of the sales force. Appointment is for a one-year term. At the end of each year, the members evaluate each other and the four members with the lowest evaluations are replaced.

The Sales Board is assigned to work only on problems with significant profit potential for the company. New product ideas are one of the assignments. The Sales Board meets face-to-face twice a year for week-long periods. The rest of the year, the Board communicates by letter and telephone. Since this is a high visibility position, members tend to make maximum contributions. What McCormick has done is to create an in-house consulting group with considerable expertise.

UTILIZING EXTERNAL SOURCES

There are also sources of ideas outside of your company, and *inventors* are one of them. The task is to make your interest known. There are basically two types of organizations that can help you; inventors associations and invention brokers. There are also specialty publications. Some of the more important ones are listed in Table 6.

USING INDUSTRY ANALYSIS

Industrial product manufacturers often conduct analyses of sales growth in industrial product categories in which they have an interest in order to identify rapidly growing markets. You can conduct your own industry analysis, or, as it is increasingly likely, purchase it from outside suppliers.

In the U.S., the U.S. Department of Commerce, Bureau of the Census, Washington, D.C. 20233 provides a wealth of data on industrial product category sales.

There are three series of reports of particular interest. *Census of Manufacturers, 1982; Annual Survey of Manufacturers* (covers years in between the census); and a series called *Current Industrial Reports* (which provides annual, quarterly and sometimes monthly data on selected industries, e. g., Clay Construction Products).

It is likely that such data are available at your local university library. Most industrialized countries have similar data available, usually through the Department of Statistics.

REVIEWING DATA CLASSIFICATIONS

It will be helpful to review how these data are organized. The basic method of organization in the U.S. is the *Standard Industrial Classification* (SIC) system. (In other countries, SITC codes do essentially the same job with somewhat different details.) SIC codes are the numerical system which subdivides all U.S. businesses into more detailed product industries or market segments. The SIC coding system first divides the nation's overall economy into 10 basic industries and assigns each a two-digit code. The basic industry groups are:

A. Agriculture, Forestry and Fishing
B. Mining
C. Construction
D. Manufacturing
E. Transportation, Communications, Electric, Gas and Sanitary Services
F. Wholesale Trade
G. Retail Trade
H. Finance, Insurance and Real Estate
I. Services
— Non-classifiable Organizations

Associations

American Society of Inventors, Inc.
1016 47th Street
Philadelphia, PA 19143

Institute of American Inventors
635 F Street NW
Washington, DC 20004

Inventors Assistance League, Inc.
1815 West 6th Street
Los Angeles, CA 90057

The Inventors Association
Box 281
Swift Current
Saskatchewan
Canada S9H 3V6

Inventors Club of America
1592 Main Street
Box 3799
Springfield, MA 01101

Brokers and Publications

American Bulletin of International
　　Technology Transfer
International Advancement
5455 Wilshire Blvd., Suite 1009
Los Angeles, CA 90036

Arthur D. Little, Inc.
Invention Management Group
Acorn Park
Cambridge, MA 02140

Table 6. Some outside sources for inventions

Manufacturing, for example, has 20 two-digit codes (20 to 39), each of which represents a Major Group such as Food: SIC 20. These, in turn, are subdivided into 143 three-digit Industry Groups, such as Dairy Products: SIC 202. The next level of detail is the Specific Industry, e. g., Creamery Butter: SIC 2021; or Fluid Milk: SIC 2026.

The next level assigns Product Classes. For example, Oil Field Machinery: SIC 3533 has four product classes.

3533 1 Rotary Oil Field and Gas Field Drilling Machinery and Equipment

3533 2 Other Oil Field and Gas Field Drilling Machinery

3533 3 Oil Field and Gas Field Production Machinery and Equipment (except pumps)

Batelle Development Corp. 505 King Avenue Columbus, OH 43201	Control Data Technote, Inc. 8100 34th Avenue South Minneapolis, MN 55440
Eurosearch Marketing Inc. 633 Fifth Avenue New York, NY 10022	Inside R&D Technical Insights 158 Linwood Plaza P.O.Box 1304 Fort Lee, NJ 07024
Interplant GM Postfach 150 246 1000 Berlin 15 Federal Republic of Germany	International New Product Center Newsletter P.O. Box 37C Esher Surrey KT10 OQN United Kingdom
Technology Mart Thomas Publishing Company One Penn Plaza New York, NY 10001	
Technology Transfer Times Ben Will Publishers 167 Corey Road Brookline, MA 02146	Selected Business Ventures New Product New Business Digest General Electric Company 1 River Road, TMO Eric Blvd. Schenectady, NY 12345

Table 6. Continued

3533 4 Other Oil Field and Gas Field Machinery and Tools
(except pumps), Including Water Well

The last level of subdivision is Products. SIC 3533 1 contains
twelve specific products.

35331 11 Christmas tree assemblies

13 Casing and tubing heads and supports

15 Chokes, manifolds and other accessories

19 Rodless pit lifting machinery and equipment (except
pumps)

53 Pumping units and accessories, including back crank
equipment

55 Other surface rod lifting machinery and equipment

57 Rod lifting equipment, subsurface (except pumps)

61 Packers

65 Screens, tubing and catchers

71 Oil and gas separating, metering and treating equipment

81 Parts for oil and gas field machinery and tools, sold separately, including parts for portable drilling rigs but excluding parts for other drilling equipment

98 Other oil and gas field production machinery and tools

As you can see, at the six-digit level, the data are quite detailed and can provide the basis for quite powerful analysis.

The data that are reported will be Total Value of Products Shipped, expressed in current dollars. That means that these data will have to be adjusted for inflation.

"Sales & Marketing Management" magazine publishes these data at the four-digit level, by state and by county, in its annual *Survey of Industrial Purchasing Power*. (Sales & Marketing Management, 633 Third Ave., New York, NY 10017).

PURCHASING A COMMERCIAL ANALYSIS

Another alternative is to purchase an industry analysis from a commercial source. These reports range in price from a few hundred dollars to over $1,000. The advantages include time and amount of detail.

Find/SVP, 500 Fifth Avenue, New York, N. Y. 10019 is a good source. On the opposite page is an explanation of one of its reports.

Predicasts, Inc., 11001 Cedar Avenue, Cleveland, OH 44106 is another source of prepared industry analyses. Either company will prepare a custom report to your specifications if a general report covering your interests is not available.

Be sure to note the publishing date for the report you are considering buying. The most recent data in the report has to be at least a year earlier than the publication date. In this fast-changing world, out-of-date data can be dangerous to your financial health.

ANOTHER AVENUE—TECHNOLOGY ANALYSIS

Another source of new product ideas lies in analyzing the changing technology in your industry and those industries you'd like to be in. Technology is always changing at some rate. The task is to identify the nature of the most probable changes and the kinds of new products that such changes will require.

The trade press in the appropriate industry is a good place to begin. Start clipping articles about how the products or the manufacturing processes or the raw materials are changing, or are expected to change. When you think you have a reasonable data base, write a summary of what you think the changes are most likely to be. Circulate your summary to your key people, along with copies of the raw data. Ask for a thoughtful review. In about two weeks, hold a meeting with those people and see if you can come to an agreement about the nature and direction of the major changes. Assign small groups to each change and ask them to think about the implications of needed new products.

In two weeks, hold another meeting and let each group present its ideas to the full group for discussion. The ones that look good become ideas for new product concepts and advance to the next stage in the process. When you have covered the major changes, go back to the minor changes and do the same thing.

Once you have the process working so that you are comfortable with it, plan to repeat it on an annual basis. Begin to build up a systematic process for generating a stream of new product ideas.

In 1980, DuPont's external house organ devoted a whole issue to the changing technology of American cars. It concluded that the major changes in American cars during the 1980's were going to be (in no special order):

- Electronic engine controls
- Front wheel drive
- Reduced maintenance
- Improved quality
- Aerodynamic styling
- Fuel economy

If you are interested in any part of the U. S. auto market and would like to get a free copy of the complete analysis, write to James Murphy, Editor, Context E. I. DuPont de Nemours & Co. (Inc), Wilmington, DE 19898. Ask for No. 3/1980, Vol.9, No. 3, Special Report—The New American Car.

Figure 13 gives you a chance to develop your own skills in technology analysis.

THE IMPORTANCE OF ENVIRONMENTAL ANALYSIS

Just as every industry operates with certain technology, every industry also operates within some environmental conditions. These environmental constraints are changing faster than the technology in many industries. A changing environment can generate new product opportunities.

To give yourself a small example of how technology analysis can lead to new product ideas, do this little exercise. Listed below are seven widely shared observations about U.S. mail service. You can do the exercise whereever you are because they are true of just about all government mail services.

The only differences are degrees of magnitude, not direction. Think about what it will mean when all of these trends converge. Write down a brief description of the major changes that are likely to occur and list the implications. Then think up three new products that will be required if your analysis comes true. Don't worry about details. "A _____ that will _____ so that _____," is close enough.

- The rapid increase in the first class postage rate will continue, reaching 50¢ by 1989 at the least.
- The cost of electronic mail system hardware and transmission will continue to decline.
- The demand for speedy exchange of messages will continue to grow.
- The use of personal computers in both home and office will continue to grow; 65% of offices and 30% of homes to have them by 1989.
- Businesses will reach a point where they cannot handle further cutbacks in mail or live with further price increases.
- Dissatisfaction with the _____ Postal Service will continue to rise.
- Electronic mail service networks such as GTE's Telemail will continue to expand.

Figure 13. A personal worksheet for technological analysis

What is all of this likely to mean?

_____

_____

_____

_____

Description of New Product #1

_____

_____

_____

Description of New Product #2

_____

_____

_____

Description of New Product #3

_____

_____

_____

Figure 13. Continued

Environmental analysis operates very much like technology analysis. Identify those parts of the changing environment that have the greatest impact on your industry. Then follow the steps outlined under technology analysis.

For example, water is rapidly changing its position in the environment. It is becoming scarce, the quality is dropping and the price is rising as the energy cost for transporting it rises. These changes are leading to change in markets like those in the following box.

Consumers: The International Bottled Water Assn. says bottled water is the fastest growing drink in the U.S. and that sales have grown 100 percent in the past four years, with no slowdown in sight.

Cities are having difficulty raising money to replace aging water distribution systems. Households are beginning to buy point-of-use purification systems.

Agriculture: In California, the fruit and vegetable basket for the entire U.S., 90 percent of the water used by the state is used for agriculture. Water for agricultural use has always been priced below cost, which has led to extremely wasteful use in growing crops. As the government finds itself under increasing pressure to increase revenues, the price of agricultural water is bound to increase. Farmers will have to learn to use water more efficiently.

Industry: More legislation is being passed to force improved treatment of industrial waste water. The chlorine and chloro-amine type by-products that are currently widely used in water treatment are suspected carcinogens.

Some industries are beginning to purify and re-cycle waste waters. Reverse osmosis membrane type systems are proving to be effective for this purpose and, occasionally, provide a bonus in the form of valuable by-products recovered.

These are just a few of the ramifications of the changing role of water in the environment. The direct new product opportunities are many, but there are also indirect opportunities.

ANOTHER ANALYSIS—SOCIAL TRENDS

Consumer products companies in particular can use the techniques discussed above to examine changing social trends. Some examples follow.

After analyzing trends in the numbers and proportions of working wives in the United States, Hal Hylton, president of Spaghetti Pot Investments, Costa Mesa, California, concluded that there was need for well-cooked food that *could be taken home to eat*. The company's Spaghetti Pot restaurants serve only spaghetti, meat sauce or meatballs, salad, cheese and garlic bread. The food is ready to go two minutes after it is ordered. The restaurants are located near supermarkets where women are likely to shop on their way home from work. They are only open from 4 p.m. to 9 p.m.

The Stouffer Foods Division of Nestle, Inc., the multinational Swiss food company, studied the trends toward single person households. The company decided there was an opportunity for single serving food products that was not being met.

Accordingly, it developed a line of frozen Italian sandwiches to be sold through supermarkets. Inside each box, the filling and sauce are packed in one container while the bread is wrapped separately. The consumer finishes cooking and preparing the sandwich at home.

Birds Eye Foods Limited watched the growth of home freezer ownership in the United Kingdom very carefully as it grew from 2 percent in 1969 to 40 percent of all households by 1979. As the market grew, Birds Eye stepped up its new product development activities and now introduces as many as 20 new frozen food products there every year.

Xerox has analyzed the changing composition of the U.S. work force to search for new product ideas. The "white collar" work force has grown to 52 percent of the total and managers are estimated to represent 75 percent of the cost of this segment.

In spite of those facts, very little was being done to improve the productivity of those expensive managers. To meet this opportunity, Xerox is currently developing "intelligent" work stations for managers by combining computers and word processors wired into a local network. It is calling this developing system Ethernet.

SEARCHING OTHER COUNTRIES FOR IDEAS

There are still surprisingly large gaps in communications among countries. It may be worth your while to visit some other countries to search for new product ideas that you could develop at home, or perhaps import or license.

Here are three examples of products that would have appeal in other countries but are, as of this writing, only marketed in the country where they were developed.

In Ireland, there are frozen chips of whipping cream packaged much like frozen vegetables. The consumer thaws out only as much as is needed.

In the United Kingdom, a powdered, dry, shelf-stable (and needing no refrigeration) yogurt is marketed. The consumer adds the powder to milk and makes up as much yogurt as he needs.

Growers in New Zealand have developed a variety of apples called Gala that have a very different pear/apple taste. They could form the basis for a number of new products.

TAPPING YOUR OWN CUSTOMERS FOR IDEAS

The unifying theme to the new product development process presented in this manual is that the new products that are most likely to be successful are those that fill unmet customer needs, i.e., products that are "market driven." All of the methods for generating new product ideas that have been discussed so far, and those yet to come, are designed to uncover such needs.

Those methods are generally indirect. Many companies maintain direct contacts between their new product development people and their customers. You should consider very seriously establishing such a program with your customers. It can pay off very handsomely.

In 1958, Warner-Lambert, Inc., the large Morris Plains, New Jersey, drug manufacturer, discovered that physicians were prescribing two different medicines for sinusitus—an analgesic and a decongestant. Warner-Lambert recognized a need for a single product so they combined a pain reliever, a decongestant and a mild antihistaminic and introduced Sinutab. The sinus-headache market in U.S. is a $50 million market, and Sinutab continues to dominate it.

In 1975, Savin Business Machines Corp. had revenues of $63 million and was only a very minor factor in the American office copier market. At that time, four out of five plain paper copiers in use in the U.S. were from Xerox.

Savin, however, had been talking to its customers. Some of them indicated that they didn't need the high quality copies that Xerox machines produced. They didn't need the speed that Xerox machines afforded. And especially they didn't need Xerox prices.

In November, 1975, Savin introduced a copier that produced less than 40 copies per minute using a liquid toner technology and carrying a substantially lower price. Two years later, Savin's revenues were in excess of $200 million and it owned a 40 percent share of the low price copier market.

These are just two examples—from thousands—of new products that were successfully developed because companies listened to their customers. There are no guidelines for how you should set up a customer listening program.

Some companies do it as informally as holding regular lunch appointments to listen to customers' business problems. Others invite selected customers and pay expenses to work sessions in vacation locations. Still others maintain specialist groups that are available to customers to solve their immediate problems.

VIII

More Sophisticated Methods for Generating New Product Ideas

The nine methods for generating new product ideas already discussed (your own employees, internal sales force, inventors, industry analyses, technological analyses, environmental and social trends' analyses, other countries, your customers) are all within the capabilities of most executives regardless of background, training or experience. They can be used by any company of any size provided there is an industrious, imaginative individual to carry them out.

The next five methods (focus groups, expert panels, market segmentation, items by use, perceptual mapping) require more skilled professional expertise. Any intelligent manager could try his hand at executing any of them, but the risk of using them ineffectively, or much worse, being misled by them increases. In either case, the chances for success go down and that's what we are trying to avoid.

If you work for a large company, it's best to involve your marketing research department. If you work for a company without a marketing research department, you should be prepared to budget for outside assistance.

The methods considered in this Section may become technically complex. The purpose here will be to avoid the complexity while giving you sufficient grasp of the technique to determine whether it is of interest to you. It will enable you to reasonably discuss your objectives with an experienced professional.

FOCUS GROUP INTERVIEWS

This research method involves gathering together a small group, usually eight to 10 people, who all possess some characteristic of interest to you. Usually the group members are customers, or potential customers, of a product category.

The interview is conducted in a meeting room under relaxed circumstances. Members are recruited in some systematic way from some larger population, and are usually paid some small amount to ensure that they actually show up for the interview.

A moderator leads the interview and follows an outline agreed upon in advance. Focus group interviews generally last for two hours. They are generally tape recorded and/or video taped for subsequent analysis. The research methodology was originally based on clinical psychology and over the years has been altered and tailored for use in marketing.

Focus group interviews help you to understand behavior patterns, attitudes and the underlying attitude structure. They are an excellent device for obtaining initial reactions to concepts and product proposals. They are also valuable in the prototype development stage.

It is highly unlikely that focus group interviewing will generate new product ideas by itself. It is a waste of time to ask a group of customers what new products they want. They don't know because they don't buy products, they buy benefits or solutions to problems. And *that* is the key to how focus group interviewing is useful in generating ideas. It lets you explore the problems that customers have in doing some job or other. It helps you to understand why they have problems, and gives you some insight into how important those problems are.

A SPECIFIC EXAMPLE OF FOCUS GROUP INTERVIEWING

City National Bank is a middle sized bank headquartered in Beverly Hills, California. Based on a number of other factors about the market for banking services, the management of City National Bank determined that the best potential strategy was to attempt to build its own business on small and medium sized businesses. They hired a research firm to conduct a series of focus group interviews with the financial officers of some small and medium sized local businesses, e. g. retailers and manufacturers.

The research found that, in general, the financial officers were quite satisfied with the level and the number of services provided by their current banks. In short, no opportunities developed for new banking services to meet unmet needs.

However, one fact that did emerge among virtually all the officers was an intense dislike for the times when they had to go to the bank to transact business. They felt that they didn't get much more attention than an individual checking account customer who walked in off the street. They also felt that the amount of business they brought to the bank warranted better treatment than that. At the same time, they realized that their businesses were not major customers of the bank and therefore not likely to get preferential treatment. They accepted the situation with resignation because there didn't seem to be anything to do about it.

City National Bank's management reviewed these findings and came up with the concept of "The Bank That Comes To You." They worked out a program built around junior bank officers, managing portfolios of business accounts, who actually went out to the customer's place of business on call. They promoted the service selectively via direct mail. The program was very successful.

RECEIVING DIRECTION FROM FOCUS GROUP INTERVIEWS

The kind of help that focus group interviews is most likely to provide is in giving you directions to pursue internally. You can sit down with your R&D people or other managers and say, "Here's what seems to be the problem. What can we do about it?"

New product people at Hunt-Wesson Foods conducted a series of focus group interviews with women on the subject of frying.

They told the R&D people that "Women tell us they like to pan fry with butter, especially eggs, but butter burns so easily that they are likely to burn the food and look like poor cooks to their families. What can we do about it?"

R&D's eventual answer was to add a butter flavor and yellow color to regular soybean-based cooking oil. Buttery Flavored Oil was introduced as a frying medium that smelled like butter, tasted like butter, but didn't burn. Buttery Flavored Oil became a very profitable product in the company's line. In general, focus group interviews offer these advantages:

- They approximate real-life interactions. Groups can be emotionally provocative because members stimulate and interact with one another. Disclosure by one encourages disclosures by others.

- Flexibility allows the moderator the freedom to pursue relevant avenues and insights. Contingencies can be handled in groups. The moderator follows a guide, not a rigid questionnaire.

- Group reports and analysis stimulate creative thinking because customer motivations and language are better understood. You gain insights into the dynamics of the product use situation.

WRAPPING UP FOCUS GROUP INTERVIEWS

You must remember two things when using focus group interviewing. One is that the moderator is *very* important. Make sure that your moderator is both skilled and experienced. He should be thoroughly briefed about your product category and your objectives before the project starts. Talk to your moderator after each interview. Decide on any changes that might be useful in the moderator's guide for remaining interviews. Don't accept just a written report at the end of the project. After you have circulated the written report to your key internal managers, hold a meeting with them and the moderator to review the results and consider any new ideas that may come up.

Second, never conduct less than three focus group interviews in a project. You are working with very small samples of your customers. The samples were only drawn for convenience. If you only do two focus group interviews you may find that each group tends to point you in a somewhat different direction without any indication of which direction is the more important. The third group tends to resolve that question. The third group increases your sample size and provides a greater overall richness and depth to the total project. Never do just one focus group interview.

THE EXPERT PANEL

This method builds on the fact that knowledge is growing explosively. The best estimates are that the total body of knowledge is doubling every 10 years. No individual can keep up with that kind of increase. Even the collective knowledge of everyone in your company is limited and distorted.

The expert panel focuses the best and most appropriate current knowledge on specific problems. It brings together a group of experts who are most likely to possess the knowledge necessary to point you in the right direction. Not every industry is moving at the same rate of change. The expert panel will be more valuable in high technology industries and others where the rate of change is rapid.

REAPING THE BENEFITS OF AN EXPERT PANEL

You should incorporate a number of steps to get the most benefit from using an expert panel. Other than these steps, the details of the actual execution vary widely to suit the situation.

First, you want to select someone outside your company to help you. There are management consulting firms, individual consultants or perhaps a professor from a local university. Interview several. Make sure they understand clearly what you expect. Note whether they make suggestions to improve the project or simply accept it as a simple assignment. Remember that you will be working closely for an extended period of time, so select someone compatible.

The main reason you want to work with an outsider is to keep your company identity from being disclosed, at least in the early stages of the project. Experts are human, too. It is quite likely that if they know you work for John Deere & Co., they will want to help you develop new farm tractors. And that may not be your purpose. Later on in the project, when the focus has been sharpened considerably, it may be useful to identify the sponsor.

Once you select a consultant, the next task is to clearly develop your objectives, break down the task into its most logical parts and identify the kinds of experts that will be most useful. The objectives will grow out of your new product development guidelines.

An example of a specific objective would look like this:

To identify as many effects as possible that 50 cents per ounce first class postage rates would have on *business* and to generate as many solutions to those problems as possible.

Then you need to break down the objective into its most important components so you can specify the kinds of expert knowledge you want to use. With this particular objective, a reasonable place to begin would be by asking how businesses use first class mail. For example:

- Some businesses use it to communicate with employees who are not stationed at the home office.
- Some businesses use it to generate revenues, e. g., direct mail houses.
- Some businesses use it to transfer funds.
- Most businesses use it to communicate with other businesses.

Next you could ask what alternatives there are to those uses.

- What are the alternative ways of communicating with employees? Advantages? Disadvantages?
- What are the alternative ways to reach prospective customers? Advantages? Disadvantages?
- What are the alternative ways to transfer funds? Advantages? Disadvantages?
- What are the alternative ways for businesses to transfer documents to other businesses? Advantages? Disadvantages?

USING THE EXPERT GUIDANCE

As the answers to these questions develop, you can see the possibilities for expert knowledge. In this example, transferring money seems to be an important function. Could you use an expert in electronic funds transfers between banks? Or should it be a banking expert? Would a direct marketing expert be helpful? Is that a direction compatible with the expressed guidelines? Should you have a small package handling specialist? Or someone with a lot of knowledge about United Parcel Service, for instance? How about the government? What will its response be to all of this? Do you need an expert on government, especially the Post Office?

You should be able to identify five or six specific areas where expert knowledge is likely to provide useful inputs. Your consultants' job is then to come up with a list of such experts who could serve on your panel. Review the selections and their backgrounds with the consultant. Indicate your first and second choices. His role is then to contact the experts and gain their cooperation.

THE FIRST MEETING OF THE EXPERTS

Next, you and the consultant need to prepare the background materials. The purpose of these materials is to focus the experts' attention, but not so narrowly as to preclude possibly useful areas. The materials should bring the experts up on the learning curve. Overall, the document should approximate how you want the course of the first meeting to run. Which things first? Which second? Any side issues of relevance?

You want them to study those background materials which you will supply and then spend a day together thinking and talking about the objectives. That meeting should be held away from your offices. A hotel or motel where you won't be disturbed is a usual choice. It may take some juggling to find a location and a date that will fit all of your experts.

The consultant moderates the meeting itself. The objective is to generate as many problems and as many solutions as possible. You don't need analysis of the value of ideas or criticism or negative comments. As you go along, you want the group to build on each other's ideas. Remember the creative process. It involves taking dissimilar concepts and re-assembling them in new ways. Use the experts to do this. The key question to repeat is, "Could this be done another way?"

Make sure that the meeting room has lots of large display space, blackboards, easels, jumbo art pads, etc. Write down key problems and solutions for everyone to see. Tape record the session.

When the meeting is over, take all of the best ideas and write short descriptions. Then gather your own group of key new product development people and examine each of the ideas one at a time. Use the same building process. Eliminate those ideas that for some clear reason could not be done by your company. Add some polish to the rest.

You now have a collection of ideas that seems to fit the market and your company. You can either send them directly to screening, or you can go through another session with the outside expert panel followed by a second internal polishing.

MARKET SEGMENTATION

Markets are almost never homogeneous and uniform. They are composed of segments with differing characteristics and differing requirements. All of these differing segments, however, must use the array of products currently on the market. That is what makes market segmentation so attractive in new product development. If you can identify segments whose needs are not being fully satisfied by the existing product array, you have a strong direction for your new product development activities (providing, of course, that the segment is large enough to economically support a business).

There are no specific rules for how you go about segmenting a market. It involves as much creativity and insight as anything discussed so far. Here are some ways in which markets have been segmented.

Consumer Products

Marketing Conditions
    Channels of distribution
    Amount of competition
    Effectiveness of advertising
    Importance of service
    Information needs

Industrial Products

Organizational
Characteristics
Industry
Location
Size
Production configuration

Consumer Products

Buyer Behavior
  Amount of product consumed
  Previous use of product
  Loyalty to product
  Motives to purchase
  Satisfaction with product
  Price

Demographics
  Age
  Sex
  Marital status
  Family composition
  Family size
  Occupation of heads of household
  Education of heads of household
  Family income
  Home ownership

Psychological Patterns
  Intelligence level
  Personality characteristics
  Hobbies
  Political attitudes

Geographic
  Location
  Population density
  Climate

Industrial Products

Technology
Profitability
Buying procedures

Purchase/Use Characteristics
  Application
  Importance of purchase
  Volume purchased
  Frequency of purchase
  Number of people influencing
    purchasing
  Choice criteria

Needs/Preferences
For Product
Characteristics
  Performance requirements
  Assistance from supplier
  Brand preferences
  Desired features
  Quality level
  Service requirements

SURVEYS FOR SEGMENTATION

With the exception of some industrial market characteristics where government data provide segmentation, you need to develop original data. This requires a formal survey using random sampling techniques. The parameters of the sample are those who use the product category. The basic data that the survey must develop are likes and dislikes about existing products, and a variety of segmentation characteristics. When the likes and dislikes data are cross-tabulated against the segmentation characteristics, new product opportunities, if there are any, should appear at the intersections.

To put it another way, you will be looking for tendencies, since results from such surveys are rarely, if ever, "clean." Suppose 13 percent of the total sample complained that Product X was not nutritious. But among women ages 24 to 35 years with chldren, 61 percent made that complaint. Here you clearly have a market segment with an unsatisfied need. (Note that 39 percent of women 24 to 35 with children *did not* make that complaint.) You have a beginning, a direction.

A good example of market segmentation was what Savin Business Machines did to segment the market for plain paper copiers in terms of performance requirements. Every copier customer simply did not have to have 100 copies per minute.

Subaru of America has defined the market segment for its cars as the economical, front-wheel drive subcompact segment. This segment can be defined as men (57%), married (67%), with a median income of $24,400 and a median age of 33 years. Subaru's products and advertising are carefully designed to reach this segment with the benefits desired.

AN EXTENSIVE SEGMENTATION SURVEY

A 1980 study of American households defined four segments in terms of attitudes about nutrition and diet. They were:

> The Casuals—The largest group, they try for a balanced diet, but they don't place a major emphasis on it (25% of all households).
>
> The Cavaliers—They eat exactly what they like and don't worry about it (21% of all households).
>
> The Calorie Watchers—These people are primarily concerned with weight control (12% of all households).
>
> The Serious—They are seriously committed to nutrition and a nutritious diet (15% of all households).

The profile of these groups appears in Figure 14 for some selected segmentation characteristics.

Profile		Attitudes Toward Diet			
SEX	TOTAL SAMPLE	CAVALIERS	CASUALS	CALORIE WATCHERS	SERIOUS
Women	74%	63%	76%	82%	76%
Men	26	37	24	18	24
Family Status					
Single	10%	11%	9%	13%	11%
Married	70	67	72	71	66
Widowed/ divorced separated	20	22	19	16	23
Race					
Nonwhite	11%	10%	8%	15%	18%
Socioeconomic Status					
Low	30%	44%	25%	20%	37%
Medium	43	36	45	49	40
High	27	20	30	31	23
Level of Knowledge About Nutrition					
Very well informed	16%	11%	14%	19%	24%
Fairly well informed	56	49	60	58	50
Not that well informed	28	40	26	23	26
Level of Concern About Additives In Food Products					
High Level	33%	14%	33%	40%	50%
Moderate Level	33	34	34	39	25
Low Level	34	52	33	21	25

1. In your own words, describe the *Serious* market segment:

_____

_____

Figure 14. A real example of segmentation results

2. Briefly describe a new food product that might appeal to the *Serious* segment:

_____

_____

Figure 14. Continued

ITEMS BY USE

This is a conceptually simple technique for examining markets for "missing" products; in practice it's a sophisticated technique and may require computer processing.

The basic concept in items by use is that people will react to new objects in terms of similarity to familiar objects. Thus, the primary task is to determine how consumers see existing products.

The first thing that you need is a working definition of the market or product category of interest. "Leisure activities," "cold beverages," "nutritious snacks," or "easy auto care" are examples. Then you survey a small group of users of the product category ($\mp$ n = 25), scattered throughout the market. Ask them to list all the products that fit that description, all the uses to which they put those products, and products which they *could* use for the same purposes.

When these data are tabulated, you have a list of products and uses that:

1. Shows the major products that comprise the bulk of the product category;
2. Shows some minor products that might have interesting characteristics;
3. Shows the major end uses which account for the bulk of the product use in this category;
4. Includes a few idiosyncratic uses that may provide insights.

Another group about the same size as the first is then shown the list of end uses and asked whether they think each of the products is suitable for that end use. These results are arranged in a matrix with products arrayed down the side and uses across the top, as in Figure 15.

Figure 15. An items by use matrix

Items (columns, left to right):
Bufferin · Sucrets · Vicks Inhaler · F & F Cough Drops · Hot Lemonade · Dristan Vaporizer · Listerine Lozenges · Vicks Cough Drops · Chloroseptic Lozenges · A Hot Toddy · Mentholatum · See the Doctor · Contac · Cough Syrup · Primatene Spray · A.P.A. Pain Relievers · Vicks Formula 44 · Bromo Seltzer · Hot Tea · Smith Bros. Cough Drops · Coriciden · Dristan Tablets · Vicks VapoRub · Fruit Juice · Aspirin · Vitamins · Ear Drops · Tetrazets · Murine Eye Drops · Vicks Nasal Spray · Salt Water Gargle · Exedrin · Romilar · Cepocal Lozenges

Uses (rows):
When you have a stuffy nose · When you have a headache · When you have minor muscle aches · When you have a tightness in your chest · When the children have a fever · When you can't breathe · In the winter when you have a sore throat · When you have a hangover · When you have a post nasal drip · When you have a cough · When you have indigestion · When you feel weak · After you've been ill · During the flu season · When the children are sick · When you have a runny nose · When you have a back ache · In the summer when you have an ear-ache · When you are nervous · When you have taken a chill · When you have sinus trouble · When you have an upset stomach · When your boy (girl) friend has a cold

The first item down the left-hand margin is the product that was seen as appropriate for the most uses. The second item (moving from top to bottom) is the one that got the second most frequent number of mentions. Continue down the page until all the products have been placed in order.

Then look at the uses. Place the use for which the most products were seen as suitable in the first position across the top of the uses list. Then place the second most frequently mentioned use to the right of the first. Continue across the page with the third, fourth, etc. uses until all the uses have been located. Put the numbers in the matrix of people who saw each product as suitable for each use. (You can see why a computer might be useful).

ANALYZING THE MATRIX

You now have a picture of the structure of the market in which you want to introduce a new product. The matrix tells you:

1. Which products are seen as appropriate for the same uses
2. Which uses are seen as appropriate for the same products
3. Which products are seen as appropriate for what uses
4. What uses are seen as appropriate for what products

Your task is to find "empty" spaces, frequent uses for which there are few suitable products. Then prepare short written descriptions of such new products, e. g., "a light, satisfying dessert that is very nutritious." When you repeat step two (surveying a third user group), include your new product descriptions. The results will tell you how much appeal your concept has and which products it will compete with. It will also provide a basis to estimate how big a market your new concept might eventually achieve, by comparing the new product's draw with the size of the market held by existing products.

PERCEPTUAL MAPPING

Customers buy products to satisfy many needs. But in a surprisingly large number of cases, the decision of which specific brand to purchase in a product category is based on a very limited number of actual characteristics of the product. Those characteristics upon which most of the decision to buy is based are usually called "determinant attributes." Because many other dimensions of the purchase situation are common to all of the competing brands, it is not unusual to find just two determinant attributes determining a purchase.

Consider the case of retail banking. A customer choosing a bank is certainly going to be influenced by a convenient location. But in most cities there will be several banking institutions that are equally convenient. Convenient banking hours are also important, but those are usually set by the government. Services offered and interest rates paid are also of importance, but those are also subject to regulation.

Studies of how consumers select retail banks have repeatedly shown that there are two determinant attributes in this choice situation, "friendly service" and "many branches." People feel that their money is important to them and they want important treatment for it. Since they can't judge whether their money gets important treatment, they use a surrogate measurement, how they themselves are treated. Thus, friendly service becomes a determinant attribute.

Since many people are quite mobile, or think that they might be, it can be important in their decision to know that the bank they choose has many branches. If the bank has many branches, it sharply reduces the possibility of being embarassed when you get caught away from home without any money. Thus, having many branches becomes a determinant attribute.

MEASURING DETERMINANT ATTRIBUTES

The measurement that is important is *not management's* judgment about whether they have friendly service or many branches. The important measurement is the *perceptions* prospective *customers* have of individual banks in terms of whether they offer friendly service or have many branches. Scaling devices allow customers to express their perceptions. In this case, an appropriate question set might be:

> "Would you please indicate on this scale how friendly you think the service at _____ bank is?"

VERY FRIENDLY						NOT AT ALL FRIENDLY
7	6	5	4	3	2	1

A similar question can get at the perception of "many branches" to "few branches." By repeating the questions for competing banks, you develop comparative data on how prospective customers perceive all the competitors in terms of determinant attributes. If these data are plotted on a pair of axes, you can draw a *perceptual map* of the determinant attributes. In our banking example, the perceptual map might look like this:

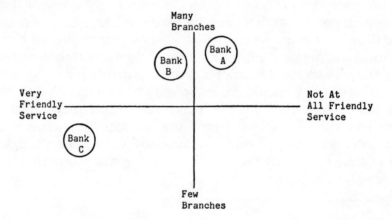

In this particular example, everyone would want to be as far up in the upper left corner as possible. Getting there is an interesting management challenge since those are basically opposing forces.

Banks with many branches have great difficulty actually delivering friendly service because the turnover among tellers is so high. The senior vice president of one major California bank described it this way; it takes three months to learn the job, three months to get bored with it and three months to find another job. On the other hand, small banks with few branches are much better able to retain employees and can do a much better job of delivering friendly service.

THE IDEAL POSITION

The lower right position in the bank example is poor, which is a good way to introduce the next idea, the notion of an "ideal" position, or "ideal" brand. In our banking example, the ideal position is obvious. For most products it is not that simple. The reason is that the opposing attributes may not represent opposing alternatives. Consider this map for a diet soft drink.

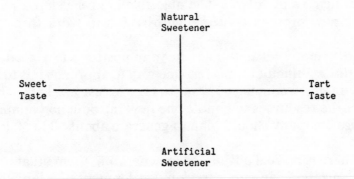

Here it is not clear what trade-offs customers would be willing to make to get their ideal product. Such situations are much more frequent than our clear-cut banking illustration.

To develop a perceptual map for the product category you are interested in:

1. Define the prospective customers.
2. Identify the determinant attributes. Use the two most important ones. It is possible to use more than two but it becomes much more complex.
3. Locate the position of the "ideal" product.
4. Locate the positions of all the major existing brands.
5. Plot the ideal brand and the competing brands on a perceptual map.

Your task is to search the map for spaces where a new product could be positioned much more closely to the ideal brand. You can use this method in industrial markets, such as supplies. Here the determinant attributes will be things like, "reliable source," "good quality," "low prices," etc.

A "PORTFOLIO" OF IDEAS

Not all these methods are appropriate for your situation, but some could prove quite useful. Most will require further modification to improve their value to you. The objective is to develop a portfolio of ideas for new product concepts with which to work throughout the year.

How many ideas to have in your portfolio is a good question, but one that is difficult to answer. One way to approach it is to ask yourself how many products you want to take to test market each year? If you have the resources to handle one new introduction annually, then an *average* company should plan to generate about 50 to 60 ideas each year.

There is no real advantage to generating them all at once, since your organization can only carry on development of a limited number of prototypes at any one time. Furthermore, if you attempt to generate all of the ideas at once, you take the risk of not screening each one thoroughly. Good ideas may get turned down and bad ideas may slip through to waste time and effort.

The best solution is to plan to generate ideas at various times throughout the year so that you can develop a stream of ideas for evaluation.

TWO OTHER SOURCES OF IDEAS

Two other sources for generating new product ideas have not been discussed here, but should be mentioned. They are consultants and brainstorming. The reason they have not been covered is that they appear to be low probability of success sources. Since good ideas can come from anywhere, that doesn't mean you should never consider them.

Consultants: There are firms and individuals who will tell you that if you hire them and give them your guidelines, they will provide you with a certain number of new product concepts that fit your guidelines. In many cases, the ideas they come back with will be shallow or wildly impractical. The reason is that they simply can't know your business as well as you do.

If someone does show up with a particularly intriguing offer, check the references! Talk to other people they have worked for. Talk to enough people in the reference company to be able to evaluate the costs versus the rewards.

Specifically, ask about the number of commercially successful products that it introduced *directly* as a result of the consultant's input. Ask for a comparison of the development costs for the consultant-generated product in relation to internally-generated idea costs.

If you still decide to go ahead, specify the results you expect very carefully and in detail. Make sure that there is a specific timetable for performance.

Brainstorming: This notion has been around for over 40 years now, and it does have some strong advocates. If this technique were as useful in new product development as its supporters claim, you'd expect that some evidence existed somewhere about the resulting successes—if not in the trade press, then at least in business folklore. If such evidence exists, it is exceptionally well concealed. You spend your money on brainstorming entirely at your risk.

THE PROBLEMS WITH UNSOLICITED IDEAS

Unsolicited ideas from people not working for your company can often induce problems, the main cause of which are "trade secrets." Such secrets have been held to have value. Therefore, if you take action after receiving an unsolicited idea that you handled improperly, you may find you have a lawsuit to deal with.

The money that you have to spend to defend yourself or to settle the suit out of court because that's less expensive than going to trial may be substantial. You should hold discussions with your legal department and work out a satisfactory procedure for dealing with unsolicited ideas.

The problem is serious enough that some companies refuse to even look at an unsolicited idea unless it has been patented. If you follow some rules for handling unsolicited ideas, you won't have to be quite that rigid. Here are four things *not* to do:

1. Simply ignore the idea and throw the letter away.
2. Write back and say that the idea is not new (even if it's not).
3. Make an evaluation of the idea, whether good or bad.
4. Write back for more information.

Instead, develop a *written company policy* with roughly these rules in it:

1. If the idea is presented orally, have the presenter write it down.
2. No matter who receives the idea, send it and any accompanying documents directly to the Legal Department. It is not to be read or evaluated in any way. The mail room should be instructed to send any envelopes marked "Attention: New Products Department," or other such notations directly to the Legal Department unopened. Secretaries and others who open mail should be instructed to stop reading as soon as they recognize the correspondence as an unsolicited idea and forward the entire package to the Legal Department.
3. The Legal Department identifies the submission in some way, such as a number, and logs in the receipt. A form letter is then sent to the submitter that outlines the conditions under which your company will consider unsolicited ideas. A waiver, or release, form is also enclosed. What the letter and waiver actually say is up to you and your legal advisor.
4. When (and if) the waiver is returned signed, the Legal Department can then forward the material to the proper person(s) for evaluation. If you are following the process outlined in this manual, the material would be forwarded to your screening group.
5. If the idea is turned down by the screening group, it is returned to the Legal Department for return to the submitter.
6. If the idea is judged to have merit, you will have to place some tentative valuation on it so that the Legal Department can negotiate some form of written contract. Nature of the contract is entirely dependent upon the situation.

7. Do not spend any further time or money on the idea until you have a written contract, signed and in your possession.

8. The exception to #6 and #7 may occur when the idea seems to have merit but you need more information to place a potential value on the idea. In that case, you may wish to negotiate a short-term option, say 60 or 90 days, for further evaluation. Some compensation to the submitter is usually paid.

9. Make sure that everybody strictly follows these rules.

This procedure does not guarantee elimination of problems. But it will certainly reduce their number. The mere existence of the system and adherence to it will discourage a substantial number of potential legal actions, and save a lot of money in the process.

A FINAL WORD ON GENERATING IDEAS

The creative process involves seeing new combinations of familiar things. Those new connections are ideas or insights. These ideas sometimes occur at inopportune moments. You may be completely engrossed in thinking about something else when the exact insight you were searching for flashes through the corner of your mind. Or, you're just falling asleep (it happens often) when the solution you were searching for is suddenly right in front of you. How do you handle such situations?

Ideas can get away from you as easily as they came. The first thing to do is *stop* whatever else you were doing. Pull over to the side of the road, get out of bed, concentrate. Write down the idea. You always want to have paper and pen nearby. Add a sketch if that helps fill out the idea. Push it as far as you can—think about sizes, shapes, colors, flavors, etc. Don't worry about judging it now. There's plenty of time for that later on.

IX

Screening New Product Concepts

You should now have a large group of ideas that fit your general guidelines, but which have had no critical evaluation. The first step to evaluate the potential of each of the ideas involves screening.

The characteristics of the concepts you choose to develop will be determined by the way that you set up your screening procedures and by the way you implement those procedures. Screening procedures must serve two directly conflicting and very difficult interests. They must be rigorous enough to ensure that the resources of the company are focused on the concepts with the best possible chances of commercial success.

But at the same time, they must not be so rigid as to unnecessarily exclude less well-defined concepts that have the potential of becoming very successful products. Furthermore, the decisions made in screening have to be made with a minimum amount of information.

One of the easiest things to do is to defer a decision for more study and more research. However, it's a luxury that you cannot afford. It is necessary to make decisions based on what you know, or think you know, and forge ahead. You can make those decisions somewhat easier by properly structuring your screening criteria.

A TWO-STEP SCREENING PROCESS

You must accomplish two different tasks in the screening procedure, and it generally works best if you keep them separate. One task is to minimize the possibility that you will devote substantial amounts of time and money to develop a project only to have to abandon it at some point in the process because it conflicts with some company policy. That is an expensive and demoralizing event, and it is important to do everything you can to avoid it.

The second task is to rank the remaining concepts in terms of their apparent attractiveness for further development. This will also include some cut-off rank that excludes a concept from any further consideration. Examination of the results at this point will show you the nature and extent of your future developmental work load. It will also give you a basis for allocating resources among the various projects and for setting up time tables.

DEVELOPING A BUSINESS POLICY CHECKLIST

You will need a list of significant factors, or business policy considerations, that would affect your new product strategy results. Since screening criteria are clearly related to your guidelines for new product development, they are the best place to start to develop your checklist. At this point, you want to identify items that can be evaluated on a simple "yes" or "no" basis.

Since the results of your new product development are an expression of the direction set for your company in your strategic plans, that is another source of items for the checklist.

While these items describe your future business policies, make sure your list includes any important constraints that are currently in place. For example, manufacturing might have a policy that anything manufactured by the company also has to be available through a co-supplier. Any item on the list that doesn't seem to be reasonably permanent doesn't belong on the list.

When you have your final checklist, prepare worksheets showing the policy items along with a place to identify the concept under consideration and to mark yes or no for each item. Call a meeting of your key people to evaluate potential policy conflicts. Present the concepts one at a time and make a group judgment about whether or not the concept fits the policy items. If a concept doesn't fit, discard it.

Once you have rejected a concept, at any stage of the screening process, walk away from it and don't worry. It's quite easy to keep saying to yourself, "Maybe if I had done it just a little differently." But that is unproductive. The reason that you have developed screening criteria is to help make decisions. Once a decision is made, don't look back.

DETERMINING CONCEPT ATTRACTIVENESS

If your guidelines are well developed, you can expect most of your concepts to advance to stage two of the screening. The objective here is to develop a list of items that determine the potential attractiveness of each concept, and to introduce more flexibility into the analysis. Each item is given a "weight" in terms of its likely contribution to the success of the product in the marketplace, and a set of evaluative criteria. For example:

ITEM	SCORE	WEIGHT
Lead time over potential competitors		
Less than one year	1	
One to two years	2	2
More than two years	3	
Annual rate of market growth		
5–9%	1	
9–15%	2	4
15% or greater	3	

If our example had only two items, a concept that would have competitors within a year (1 × 2) and was in a market growing at over 18 percent annually (3 × 4) would get a rank score of 14.

The items to use, the scoring system, the weights and the other details of stage two screening are unique to each company. There are simply no strict rules for how to do it, and that's as it should be.

However, as you develop a stage two screen, keep one rule in mind. Use items where decisions can be made based on low cost, quickly available information. This is not the time to invest substantial resources in an attempt to gain precision in your decision-making.

The point of successful new product development is to focus your resources on the best prospects. Spending at this stage diffuses your resources instead of focusing them. Another reason not to concentrate on developing precise data at this stage is that "precision" is probably an illusion. If the concept progresses all the way to commercial introduction, it will generally end up being very different from the concept. This is inescapable because compromises have to be made at every step of designing the product. The concept contains no compromises.

The one item that should *never* be in your screening item list is Return on Investment (ROI). Serious ROI calculations take time and money. They tend to be wrong because your accountants will be working with illusory data. ROI calculations do have a place in the new product development process, but this is not it.

Figures 16 and 17 show actual second stage screens used by the United Kingdom bakery goods company (mentioned in Section III) and from a California electronic products company. They are not intended as exact models to follow. They are simply examples of the ways two companies found to handle this task.

COMPARING THE SCREENING EXAMPLES

The screening procedures of these two companies are similar in concept but quite different in detail. The differences reflect the concerns of the different managements, their perceptions of their strengths and weaknesses, and their strategic goals. As was the case with guidelines, you must develop screening procedures to fit the personality and needs of your individual organization.

Two things are common to both systems and should be common to your procedures. One is that both systems allow the individual evaluator to express his best judgment about the concept in a relatively simple fashion. Both use a five point scale to accomplish this. Such scales are used frequently because they can be handled in a simple manner,

U. K. BAKERY GOODS COMPANY (CONCEPTS RATED ON 1–5 POINT SCALE)

Item	Score	Weight
1. *The Market*		
a. *Potential size in national launch year*		
£20m +	5	
£10 − 20m	4	
£3 − 10m	3	40
£1 − 3m	2	
Under £1m	1	
b. *Growth prospects* (in real terms over the next five years)		
Much faster than growth of population	5	
Faster than growth of population	4	
In line with population growth	3	40
Static	2	
Declining	1	
c. *Susceptibility to economic fluctuations*		
Strong demand, independent of economic climate	5	
Reasonably stable demand	4	
Slightly sensitive to economic conditions	3	20
Fairly sensitive to economic conditions	2	
Very sensitive to economic conditions	1	
2. *The Product*		
a. *Consumer distinction*		
Superior and difficult to imitate	5	
Superior but imitatable	4	
Slightly better, plus gimmick	3	60
"Me-too" plus gimmick	2	
Completely "me-too"	1	
b. *Consumer appeal*		
Easily understood concept with wide appeal	5	
Easily understood concept with minority appeal	4	
Some communication problems	3	40
Difficult concept but wide relevance	2	
Difficult concept with minority relevance	1	

Figure 16. A screening device used by a United Kingdom bakery

3. *Competition*	Score	Weight
a. *Competitive advertisers*		
Market split between several unsophisticated companies	5	
Market split between two or three unsophisticated companies	4	
One major competitor only	3	40
Market split between two major companies	2	
Three or more major competitors	1	
b. *Own label competition*		
Nil	5	
Some	4	
Average	3	25
High	2	
Dominating	1	
c. *Price flexibility*		
Considerable freedom	5	
Consumer price sensitivity low	4	
Consumer price sensitivity high	3	25
Highly competitive with price as a major factor	2	
No freedom (e.g., government control)	1	
4. *The Company*		
a. *Product compatibility*		
Strongly complementary to existing products	5	
Fairly complementary to existing products	4	
No interaction with existing products	3	20
Fairly competitive with existing products	2	
Strongly competitive with existing products	1	
b. *Company strength*		
Dominant position in market	5	
Company strength will help launch	4	
Company strength will neither help nor hinder	3	20
Company lacks strong presence in market	2	
Company unfamiliar with marketing/sales/distribution	1	

Figure 16. Continued

c. *R & D*	Score	Weight
Product advantage from unique company process	5	
Product advantage from formulation expertise	4	
Adequate product resulting from general company skills	3	15
Existing facilities allow adequate product but with no competitive advantage	2	
Product type unfamiliar to R & D	1	
d. *Production*		
Can be produced on existing plant with spare capacity	5	
Can be produced on existing plant	4	
Capable of production on existing plant	3	15
Significant investment required	2	
Major capital investment needed plus long delivery time	1	
e. *Distribution*		
Present facilities adequate	5	
Small extension required	4	
Some extension required	3	15
Large extension required	2	
Completely different outlets to be called on	1	
f. *Sales force motivation*		
Sales force capacity and strong competitive advantage	5	
Some competitive advantage	4	
Equal competition	3	15
Sales force not as good as competition	2	
Completely unsuitable	1	
5. *Financial Return*		
a. *Estimated sales (at manufacturer's price) in a going year*		
Over £3m	5	
£2m — £3m	4	
£1m — £2m	3	25
£500,000 — £1m	2	
Under £500,000	1	

Figure 16. Continued

b. *Estimated gross profit margin*	Score	Weight
Over 40%	5	
30% — 40%	4	
25% — 30%	3	35
20% — 25%	2	
Under 20%	1	
c. *Marketing investment*		
Will make a profit in Year 1	5	
Will break-even in Year 1	4	
Modest loss in Year 1, recovered in Year 2	3	20
Payout period up to 3 years	2	
Payout period over 3 years	1	
d. *Capital investment* '		
Nil	5	
Slight in relation to turnover	4	
Average in relation to turnover	3	20
High in relation to turnover	2	
Heavy in relation to turnover	1	

FINAL EVALUATION

1. The Market   _ pts.
2. The Product   _ pts.
3. Competition   _ pts.
4. The Company   _ pts.
5. Financial Return   _ pts.

TOTAL POINTS   _

Figure 16. Continued

and they allow a straightforward quantification of the judgments of a variety of people. However, there are other ways to accomplish this task. Three point scales and even bi-polar scales can also do the job.

The second point common to both procedures is the way in which financial data is treated. Finances are not ignored, but they are not treated in depth. Estimates are asked about the eventual size of the business, approximate gross margins, pay-back periods, etc. But they are the kinds of information that can convey a sense of the profit potential of the concept without forcing decimal-point accuracy.

CALIFORNIA ELECTRONICS PRODUCTS COMPANY

New Product Evaluation Matrix

CHARACTERISTIC	RELATIVE IMPORTANCE WEIGHT	RATING	VALUE
Company operations			
Compatibility	0.6	5	3.0
Safe product	0.6	5	3.0
No interruption	0.4	4	1.6
Long-range growth	1.4	5	7.0
	3.0		14.6
Potential market			
Industry growth	1.2	3	3.6
Market diversity	0.6	3	1.8
Dependence on economy	0.4	4	1.6
Seasonality	0.2	5	1.0
Geographic	0.3	5	1.5
Purchasing patterns	0.3	3	0.9
	3.0		10.4
Marketability			
Channel is cost effective	0.4	2	0.8
Promotable	0.4	4	1.6
Price-quality relationship	0.4	4	1.6
Discounts/deals	0.2	5	1.0
Marketing management	0.3	4	1.2
Customer loyalty	0.3	2	0.6
Product differentiation	0.3	5	1.5
Market life	0.2	4	0.8
Competition	0.4	4	1.6
Customer acceptance	0.4	5	2.0
Sell to present customers	0.2	2	0.4
Knowledge of customers	0.4	3	1.2
Packaging	0.1	5	0.5
	4.0		14.8

Figure 17. A screening device used by a California electronics firm

CALIFORNIA ELECTRONICS PRODUCTS COMPANY

New Product Evaluation Matrix

CHARACTERISTIC	RELATIVE IMPORTANCE WEIGHT	RATING	VALUE
Engineering/production			
Access to resources	0.4	5	2.0
Manufacturing expertise	0.5	5	2.5
Marketable cost	0.4	5	2.0
Storage requirements	0.2	5	1.0
Entry requirements	0.4	4	1.6
Serviceability	0.3	5	1.5
Durability	0.2	5	1.0
Research budget	0.2	5	1.0
By-products	0.2	5	1.0
Operating costs	0.2	5	1.0
	3.0		14.6
Finance			
Estimated profitability	1.6	5	8.0
Payback period	0.6	5	3.0
Available capital	1.0	4	4.0
Best use of capital	0.8	5	4.0
	4.0		19.0
Legal			
Patent protection	0.8	4	3.2
Meets product, label and advertising restrictions	0.8	4	3.2
Trademark protected	0.6	4	2.4
Royalties	0.2	4	0.8
Labor relations	0.2	5	1.0
Other legislation	0.4	5	2.0
	3.0		12.6

Total Score 86.0

Note: Ratings are scored on a 1 to 5 scale. 5 is excellent, 3 is average and 1 is very poor. Concepts socring 80.0 or better are considered excellent projects for development. The concept shown evaluated in this example went into prototype development.

Figure 17. Continued.

ALTERNATIVE SCREENING PROCEDURES

A two-step screening procedure is useful in highlighting the work to be accomplished in screening new product concepts, but it is not the only method you can use. Arthur D. Little, Inc., the Cambridge, Massachusetts management consulting firm, has a subsidiary that specializes in new product development. The group screens as many as 4,500 new product concepts annually, and nine out of 10 of its projects have been commercial successes.

The ADL group uses just nine criteria in its screening procedure. The items reflect the nature of the business problem, with two overriding considerations. One is simply the huge amount of work involved in screening that many ideas. The procedure must be simple and quick. The other is that ADL products are manufactured by someone else under license.

These are the criteria:

1. Market potential is in excess of $5 million annually.
2. The new product is protected by patents with no infringement or title problems.
3. The technology is sound and is an important advance, not just a modest improvement.
4. The product costs less to produce than competitive products.
5. The technology is at least at the prototype stage.
6. The new product must not have been extensively shown to prospective licensees.
7. The product should be capable of manufacture in the U.S. within two years.
8. All pertinent information must be available to ADL for evaluation.
9. The new product must be capable of evaluation for only modest amounts of time and money.

Some examples of products that have met those criteria are; a drug taken orally that reduces dental caries, an improved TV picture tube, a solar water heater, a method for recovering gold from manufacturing scrap, a water purification system for consumers, and a drug that is useful in treating a specific mental illness.

USING A MULTI-STAGE APPROACH

Some companies use a multi-stage screening process that may contain up to 10 steps. Such companies usually are trying to make their "final" screening judgments on more detailed data than we have described.

They organize the process so that the items that have the least cost for data, and are the most discriminating, come in the early stages of the process. Therefore, concepts with the least merit are eliminated early with minimum cost. This allows more resources to be devoted to developing data on the surviving concepts.

Other companies add a third stage to the two-step screening process by using focus groups (described in Section VI) comprised of prospective customers to gain additional reactions to concepts. This procedure is particularly useful for consumer products, but also has applications for industrial products.

The Agricultural Division of Ciba-Geigy Corporation, the Summit, New Jersey pharmaceutical manufacturer, uses focus groups of farmers to evaluate new product concepts as part of its screening procedure.

WRITING CONCEPT STATEMENTS

No matter what form your own screening procedures finally assume, it is important to develop a uniform method for *presenting* concepts for evaluation. You don't want to penalize a good concept through weak presentation or strengthen a poor concept by giving it a strong presentation. What you do want is a uniform method of concept presentation.

The most widely used method to convey concepts uniformly is a short written statement describing the concept. You may also want to include a visualization of the concept. If you do decide to include a

**NEW PRODUCT CONCEPT SCREENING FORM
BUSINESS POLICY**

New Concept Identification: _____

_____

Name of Evaluator: _____

Date of Evaluation: _____

Company Policy	Is Concept Compatible?		
	YES	NO	MAY BE A PROBLEM
_____	____	____	____
_____	____	____	____
_____	____	____	____
_____	____	____	____
_____	____	____	____
_____	____	____	____
_____	____	____	____
_____	____	____	____
_____	____	____	____
_____	____	____	____
_____	____	____	____

Figure 18. A screening form for business policy in new product development.

Product Planning Page 7

NEW PRODUCT CONCEPT SCREENING FORM
BUSINESS POTENTIAL

New Concept Identification:_____

_____

Name of Evaluator: _____

Date of Evaluation: _____

Instructions: Please use a five point scale (5 is best, 3 is average, 1 is worst) to evaluate this concept on each item listed below. Please multiply your ranking of each item by the Weight shown for the item to develop a score.

ITEM   WEIGHT   RATING   SCORE

Marketing Factors

_____ ____ ____ ____

_____ ____ ____ ____

_____ ____ ____ ____

Manufacturing Factors

_____ ____ ____ ____

_____ ____ ____ ____

_____ ____ ____ ____

Figure 19. A new product screening form for business potential

ITEM	WEIGHT	RATING	SCORE
R & D Factors			
_____	___	___	___
_____	___	___	___
_____	___	___	___
Financial Factors			
_____	___	___	___
_____	___	___	___
_____	___	___	___
Other Factors			
_____	___	___	___

Figure 19. Continued

visual, then you must do it for all concepts. Each concept description should include these four things:

1. A statement of the problem that the product is supposed to solve. A description of the need that you think exists.
2. A description of the solution that the new product will supply. How will it solve the problem that exists.
3. A definition of the specific attributes, or characteristics, of the new product that make the solution possible. What makes it possible for the new product to satisfy the existing need.
4. Concept statements for industrial products and services should also include an estimated price or price range.

In preparing concept statements, keep the language simple. Keep the paragraphs and the sentences short. Don't make judgments that will be better made later, e.g., the product name. *Never* exceed one typewritten page. If you can't organize a concept statement in a page, or less, it's evidence that you really don't understand the concept.

Product Planning Pages 6 and 7 in Figures 18 and 19 give you a place to begin to develop screening criteria for your company. They involve a two-step evaluation procedure. Fill them out. The final forms that you prepare will likely be different from these Planning Pages, but this will provide you with some insights about the work to be done.

X

Conducting the Business Analysis

Interesting new product concepts should now be emerging from your screening procedures. They *seem* to represent real needs in the market place and they *seem* to represent products that your company can make. All your expectations are based on assumptions which, in turn, are based on experienced judgment.

The business analysis and prototype development phases of the new product development process hold those assumptions up to reality so you can test their validity. This reality testing can confirm your assumptions, or it can cause you to modify your assumptions, or it can lead you to abandon the assumptions as inaccurate.

Although a few firms do not begin prototype development until after the business analysis has been completed, most companies do both activities concurrently. The primary reason is that both activities are done in relatively small, incremental steps that feed back information from one activity to the other.

ENVISIONING THE FINAL PRODUCT

At this stage of the development process, you simply don't know exactly what the finished product should be like. That's what you will be trying to do as you move through these two phases. You can picture what is going to happen now as twin lines (business analysis and prototype development) that are almost parallel and on a spiral that moves in ever smaller circles as you zero in on a final goal.

It is very difficult to describe this simultaneous process in writing without a lot of confusing referrals back and forth. In the interests of clarity, we will treat the topics sequentially, business analysis in this Section and prototype development in the next Section.

SIX TASKS IN BUSINESS ANALYSIS

There are six general tasks that come under the heading of business analysis. They are all interrelated and should be done at approximately the same time. They are:

1. Define the potential market in some way so that it can be measured.
2. Confirm that a need really exists for your new product concept.
3. Make sure that your concept actually matches the need; that it supplies the right benefit to the customer.
4. Establish a communication capability that accurately conveys the new product's benefit to the potential customer.
5. Begin the financial analysis to give guidance to prototype development and support for the R&D investment.
6. Set "if, then" rules. Provide clearly specified criteria, in advance, that determine whether, and under what conditions, additional time and money will be spent on the project as it develops.

The overall goal in business analysis is quite similar to screening. The objective is to take a series of measurements, with each subsequent measurement getting somewhat narrower than the previous one. The earliest measures should be inexpensive and quick so that there is more time and money to spend fine-tuning those projects that get close to test marketing status.

Remember the spaghetti sauce example from Section IV. One of the most serious mistakes was to spend virtually all of the marketing research budget on the *first* consumer taste test. Think how much differently that whole story might have turned out if the first test were a small-scale exploratory test.

The basic decision matrix should go like this. If a product concept passes a preliminary small-scale test, you go on. If a product concept fails a preliminary small-scale test, you have a choice, i.e., you can stop or you can retest under altered conditions. If a product passes a large-scale preliminary test, you go on. If a product fails a large-scale preliminary test, you have no choice! The reason that understanding this decision matrix is so important is that the odds against getting everything exactly right the first time are overwhelming.

TOOLS TO COORDINATE THESE ACTIVITIES

When you think about combining all the simultaneous activities in business analysis with all the parallel, simultaneous activities that must take place in prototype development, you probably get a growing suspicion that managing all of these activities and keeping them on schedule is complicated. It is! And each additional new product concept that you put into the process adds to the complications.

Fortunately, there are some very useful techniques to help you manage this complexity, such as Flow Diagrams, PERT (Program Evaluation and Review Technique) Charts and Critical Path Analysis. They all have their heritage in production scheduling and all can be quite useful in new product development.

A detailed discussion is beyond our purpose here, but you should be aware of these management tools. There are any number of books already published that can be helpful. In fact, somebody in your own manufacturing department is probably using one or more of them right now.

DEFINING THE POTENTIAL MARKET

There are a number of ways to define markets. Sometimes it is as simple and straightforward as SIC Code 35331 11, "companies that manufacture Christmas tree assemblies for use in oil field drilling rigs," because a new flow control device was designed specifically for that application. Sometimes it is as general as "women ages 25 to 49," because TV advertising is very important in introducing the new product and that is the tightest specification that you can use to buy TV time.

The idea of a market begins with identifying a group of customers who have the ability and the willingness to buy something. These people have a need and the means to do something about it. However, if no product exists to satisfy this need, no market exists. Therefore, markets must be defined both in terms of customers' needs and product benefits to satisfy those needs.

Potential markets are most likely to be defined in SIC Code numbers for industrial products and in terms of demographics for consumer products. Such definitions are only partial substitutes for the definition you would really like to have for the potential market—i.e. needs.

It is an absolute certainty that some customers in that SIC Code, and some customers with those demographics, have no interest in your new product at all. It is also a virtual certainty that there are customers not included in conventional market definitions that really are excellent prospects.

Never lose sight of the fact that better definitions exist, if only you can find them. One of the attractions of the Items by Use Matrix is that it lets you actually examine markets in terms of needs and products, without intervening variables. Even if the Items by Use Matrix is not useful in your business, keep the concept in mind.

CONFIRMING THAT A NEED ACTUALLY EXISTS

This task is closely related to defining markets, since the ideal definition of a market is in terms of needs. Because it is frequently too difficult to define markets in terms of needs, surrogate definitions are used and needs are blurred. Once the focus on satisfying customers' needs is lost, problems arise. Some examples will make the point clear.

Campbell Soup Company's red and white cans of condensed soup are familiar sights in many parts of the world. In looking for new markets (not new products, but a similar problem), Campbell's found that Brazil is a market where soup is a very important part of family eating. It also found a growing middle class that could afford to buy Campbell's soup products. Not unreasonably it seemed at the time, Campbell's entered the Brazilian market with a market definition focused on middle class housewives.

Within two years, Campbell's marketing and advertising in the Brazilian market had won the company a number of awards and lost the company over $2 million.

What the typical Brazilian housewife needed was a soup starter to which she could add her own flavorings and ingredients. With a dehydrated product such as they could get from Knorr or Maggi, the Brazilian homemakers could serve their families soup that was truly their own. A soup that only allowed you to add water and heat could never fill that need. Campbell's clearly failed to define the market in terms of needs.

General Mills, Inc., the Minneapolis, Minnesota food products company decided to enter the Japanese market with cake mix products, which are one of the company's important product lines. Research told General Mills that very few Japanese homes have ovens, but electric rice cookers are widely available.

Using this information, General Mills developed and introduced a line of cake mixes specifically designed to be made in electric rice cookers. It was a complete failure. Japanese women are very concerned over the purity of the rice that they serve, and would never do anything to risk contaminating the flavor.

General Mills developed a product for which no need

existed. They let a market defined in terms of appliances mislead them.

Standard Brands, Inc. is another large food products company. A major product line for Standard Brands is margarine. Growth in the market for margarine is slowing down. So Standard Brands went looking for new products it could make out of margarine.

The company developed a refrigerated bar form of gravy mix which it called Smooth & Easy. They introduced the product at the end of 1977. By the end of the following year, Standard Brands had lost over $6 million on Smooth & Easy. At one point, Standard Brands was buying back more of the product from the trade, in spoils, etc., than it was selling.

The reason for the fiasco was quite straightforward. Smooth & Easy was judged by consumers to be markedly inferior to existing products. Standard Brands developed a product to satisfy its own needs, not the customers' needs.

Hindsight is all well and good. But the real question is whether these mistakes could have been foreseen and avoided. While it can never be definitely proven, the answer is almost certainly "yes".

In each case, the companies failed to do the necessary reality testing to confirm that a need really existed for their products. Confirming that a need exists is always a very difficult task, but in these three cases nobody seems to have bothered to try to do it.

MATCHING THE CONCEPT AND THE NEED

Closely related to the question of whether a need really exists for your new product concept is the question of whether your concept actually meets that need. These are the two sides to the new product development question, i.e., finding an unmet need and developing a product to fill the need. Ensuring that your concept meets the need is just as important as ensuring that the need exists.

In the Brazilian example above, it is clear that a need existed. But the Campbell condensed soup didn't match the need. Campbell's failure to ensure that the product actually matched the need was a very expensive oversight.

Another example demonstrates both problems. An industrial products company was deeply involved in developing an electric pavement breaker to be used in place of pneumatic breakers. The engineering department was having difficulty developing sufficient power from standard 110 volt wall sockets. At the same time, the product planning group was convinced that the flexibility of being able to use any standard socket was crucial to the success of the product.

They finally decided to talk to potential customers to find out whether power or flexibility was more important. To their surprise they found that the potential customers would not be interested in an electric pavement breaker under any conditions. The concept did not fit the need. But the investigating team did find that contractors who were using sledge hammers on light duty construction break-up jobs were very interested in an electric breaker that was lighter and easier to use than a sledge hammer. Such a product is currently under development.

Confirming that a need exists and that your product concept meets that need are essentially marketing research jobs. Input from R&D is usually required to carry out such tasks. Therefore, a more detailed discussion appears in the next Section, Prototype Development. The point is that throughout your business analysis you must keep referring back to those two questions (existing need and fulfillment of that need) to make certain that you are on target. All your market and financial analyses are based on the assumption that the answer to both questions is "yes."

ESTABLISHING COMMUNICATIONS CAPABILITY

It is not enough that a need exists and that your product meets that need. You must also be able to communicate that information to prospective customers in a clear and meaningful manner. You should develop a creative communications strategy for each new product concept as soon as it passes the screening procedures. A written creative strategy serves as a guide for developing advertising and/or sales materials and as a reference point for product development. There is little point to developing an outstanding product if you cannot easily make customers understand what it will do for them.

Figure 20 shows the guidelines for developing creative strategy statements used by a large consumer goods manufacturer. With slight adaptations, you should be able to make these instructions fit your own company's situation and requirements.

PREPARING FINANCIAL NUMBERS

Central to the business analysis stage is developing tentative financial analyses. This is a part of the new product development process that must be handled VERY carefully.

In the beginning, the numbers that you will be working with will be mostly crude estimates and best guesses. In spite of the fact that you know that to be true, it is very easy for others in the company to treat your estimates as final.

On the other hand, you don't want your management to view your numbers as so indefinite that they cannot put any faith in them. Eventually you are going to ask management to "invest" company funds based on the promises of your numbers.

You should develop a consistent method to display financial information to your company's executives and make sure that they have a reasonable understanding of the basis for your numbers. As you move through each iteration of the development process, they will be able to see how the numbers are likely to become more definite as they become based on better information. If you repeat this procedure over a number of projects, top management will begin to develop its own framework for evaluating your numbers at each stage of the process.

CREATING YOUR OWN "BUILD-UP" MODEL

The best way to develop management's confidence in numbers is to use "build-up" numbers that executives can examine at each step of the way. This also allows you to tap the best experience and judgment of your top management. Table 7 provides a good basis for developing

A CREATIVE COMMUNICATION STRATEGY

The Creative Strategy statement is essentially an extension and elaboration of the product's marketing strategy principles into the product's advertising, selling and creative areas. It picks up from a creative standpoint where the marketing strategy leaves off—indicating agreed upon basic and relatively long-term selling "approaches" to the customer. Its basic function is to define clearly:

1. The total net impression which the advertising is expected to leave with a specific target group.
2. Other *basic* decisions which will shape and direct the content and form of all selling messages.

Thus, the creative strategy describes the basis upon which a product is to be distinguished from competitive products; how the product is to be positioned in the minds of the target group; or how it will be given a distinct identity of its own.

It is used as a guide in the development of advertising and as a benchmark for evaluating advertising.

Creative strategy should be thought of as long-term strategy, since one of the purposes of this statement is to give continuity to the advertising and selling program over a period of time. Basic creative strategy is ordinarily changed only when there is a fundamental change in the character of the market or the product, a major competitive threat, or demonstrated failure of the existing strategy to achieve specific objectives.

Since the creative strategy is a logical extension of the marketing objective and strategy of the product, the new product development group and the advertising agency account team are responsible for the initiation and the development of a new creative strategy.

What the Creative Strategy Includes

Every creative strategy should include the specific, basic selling idea(s) or the basic concept(s) which the product's advertising and sales material is designed to establish with the customers and, as a result, motivate him/her to purchase the product in preference to competing products.

Figure 20. One company's approach to communication strategy

The following kinds of ideas will ordinarily appear in a creative strategy, but not all of them need appear in any one statement.

1. A concise statement of the principal *benefit* offered by the product. This idea represents the basic reason customers are expected to purchase the product in preference to competitive products. It is important to note that this part of the statement is not an analysis of all possible product benefits, but represents a *decision* as to which of these benefits is/are to be emphasized in the customer communications.

2. A statement of the principal *characteristic(s)* of the product which makes it possible to claim this benefit—that is, the *"reason why"* this benefit exists and has meaning to the target group. (Examples: an ingredient, a process, a quality standard.) Stated another way, these ideas identify points of product *distinctiveness or superiority* which bear directly on the customer benefit claimed.

3. A statement of the *character or personality* which is to be built for the product and which will be reflected in the mood, tone, and overall atmosphere of the communications (long-term). Elements of such a product character might include ideas like feminine, progressive, vital, playful, conservative, wholesome, luxurious, etc.

4. A statement of *what the product is* and *what the product is used for* (where the answers to these questions are not clearly obvious). Examples: Is it a meal or a snack? a food dish or an ingredient? a beverage or a multiple use product? a basic food or a problem-solving dietetic? In short, answers to the question "where does this product fit into the customer's experience?"

As a useful exercise, try writing a creative strategy for your biggest selling product (assuming that you don't already have a creative strategy for the product).

1. The Principal Benefit

Figure 20. Continued

---

2. The Reason Why

---

3. The Product's Personality or Character

---

4. What The Product Is Used For

Figure 20. Continued

your own "build-up" model, since not all components are applicable to every business.

For example, refrigerator manufacturers aren't terribly concerned with repeat purchases. Numerical controls machinery manu-

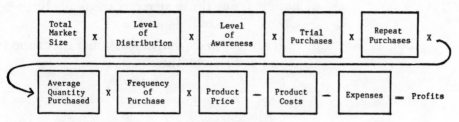

Table 7. A usable model for estimating build-up

facturers won't be overly concerned with frequency of purchase. Use the parts that apply to your new products and ignore the rest.

In the early stages of the business analysis process, it is often sufficient to show what you think the model will look like at some single point in the future, say the first year of full distribution. As you develop better data, it is often useful to show how the model looks each year for the first three to five years. This allows your management to examine the trends you expect to develop as well.

The key rule to remember in preparing the numbers is that there is nothing that top management distrusts more in new product development than a *single* sales or profit estimate. It gives them no basis for judgment and invites a rejection.

ESTIMATING TOTAL MARKET SIZE

As the project passes through successive iterations, the following sequence of forecasting total market size is not uncommon. Not every product need pass each form of forecasting, however. The sequence does hold to the general principle of using quick and inexpensive methods early and moving to more precision as the project develops.

First Attempt: Your own best estimate, usually built on some other outside frame of reference.

Second Attempt: Jury of executive opinion where you pool the best judgments of other managers in your company.

Third Attempt: Sales force survey so that you can get an evaluation from those persons most likely to be closest to potential customers.

Fourth Attempt: Survey of prospective customers' reactions and purchase intentions.

QUESTIONS FOR CONSUMER PRODUCTS

If your product is targeted to consumers, you should consider these questions.

    a. Is it a consumer durable good or a consumer packgaged good with repeat purchases?

Consumer durables are usually characterized by long intervals between purchases, relatively high unit costs, substantial lead items. Forecasting here tends to focus more on the rate of development of the total market, time-until-market saturation on the PLC and replacement rates. On the other hand, consumer packaged goods forecasting tends to concentrate on the levels of initial trial and, especially, the repeat purchasing patterns.

    b. Is the market well-defined by some easily measured characteristics, or is it difficult to define?

In well-defined markets, share of market is usually the center of forecasting interest. In ill-defined markets, forecasts should concentrate on volume.

    c. Will the product be purchased regularly throughout the year, or will purchases be irregular?

Regularly purchased consumer packaged goods are most suitable to the trial and repeat forecasts mentioned above. The really risky forecasts involve those products with irregular, or seasonal, purchase patterns. Dessert products, for instance, are notoriously difficult to forecast.

CONSIDERATIONS FOR INDUSTRIAL PRODUCTS

If you are developing industrial products—particularly high technology products—the following considerations will affect your forecasts.

- Personal relationships between vendors and customers can be very important. Many sales are made on the basis of the customer's faith in the claims and abilitites of a particular salesperson.
- It is very difficult to substitute for previous successful experience with a particular vendor. The closest thing to it is some other user's successful experience with the product in a similar situation.
- Buyers of various kinds of production machinery often prefer suppliers who have a demonstrated knowledge of the production processes involved. Technical features of the new product may not be as important when they come from suppliers who are new to the industry.
- Custom-made or relatively sophisticated equipment usually requires a period of breaking in, alteration and repair. In these cases, rapid, efficient service and support may be as important in the purchase decision as the product itself.
- Unless you can clearly demonstrate and communicate the cost-saving or profit-making potential of your new product, price may play a very large part in the decision process.

INCORPORATING LEVEL OF DISTRIBUTION CONSIDERATIONS

Whatever your estimates are of the total market, they will most likely have to be reduced to reflect the fact that very few products ever attain 100 percent distribution. In most cases, 100 percent distribution isn't even desirable because the marginal accounts are too expensive to service. If your new product will be distributed through multiple channels, then you'll need estimates for each channel. These are the distri-

bution facts facing the manufacturer of a new antacid in the U.S.
market:

WHERE CONSUMERS BUY ANTACIDS

Drug stores	61%
Supermarkets	20%
Discount stores	15%
Other stores	4%

Comparing the distribution levels of existing products, yours
and/or competitors', is a good starting place in reasonably well-defined
markets. Try to identify differences between your new product and
existing products, and make adjustments in your estimates
accordingly.

FACTORING IN OTHER CONSIDERATIONS

Level of Awareness. Whatever level of distribution your new product
achieves, it is unlikely that you be able to afford to make all of the
potential customers inside that distribution area aware of the product.
Therefore, you will have to reduce your market penetration estimates
to reflect that fact. This is a good point to do some in-depth thinking
about your introductory marketing program.

Trial Purchases. Among those potential customers who could buy
your new product both because it was available and they were aware
of it, not all will actually make a purchase. You will have to further
reduce your estimates to reflect this fact. The appropriate information
here is the proportion of the target market which expresses interest in
your creative strategy statement, either on judgment or through survey
data.

Repeat Purchases. For most consumer packaged goods, industrial supplies and certain other types of goods and services, the crucial
business question is that of repeat purchases. You will have to estimate
the proportion of customers who make a trial purchase and then go on
to become regular customers. The real answer to this question can only
be found in test marketing, but at this preliminary stage you can

extrapolate from the actual experiences of similar products that are already on the market.

Average Quantity Purchased. Now that you have some estimates of the numerical size of your potential customer base, you need to adjust that number to reflect what you expect to be the average quantity that each customer will buy. This estimate should grow out of what you know about the customers' need that you are attempting to meet.

Frequency of Purchase. When the number of customers, the average quantity purchased and the frequency with which the product is purchased are all estimated, you have a first reasonable estimate of the potential volume involved in your new business. Frequency of purchase estimates should also grow out of what you know about the customers' needs.

Product Price. When you combine your estimate of the potential volume with your first estimates of the planned selling price, you have an estimate of the potential dollar value of the new business.

Product Costs. The fact that the project got this far was based on some assumption about product costs. Use that target cost assumption in the early stages and refine your estimates as you obtain additional data from R&D as the project develops. Subtracting product costs from total dollar revenues will give you an estimate of gross margin.

Expenses. As you were thinking about the kind of marketing program that would produce the desired levels of awareness, you were undoubtedly putting a price on that program. When you subtract that and your other related distribution costs from your gross margin estimates, you finally have a projection of the profit potential your new product represents for your company.

ADDITIONAL FINANCIAL CONSIDERATIONS

Your build-up model estimates probably don't incorporate development costs or company asset investment requirements. You might get requests to develop Return on Investment (ROI) estimates.

It is in everyone's best interests to put off developing ROI estimates for as long as possible. At this stage of business analysis, ROI estimates can be both misleading and destructive. There are so many arbitrary assignments of value to tangible and intangible assets in an

ROI calculation that they can create an unsupportable load for a new product project.

Two financial tools make good sense in new product development work. You should use both because they are valuable as sensitivity analyses and as devices to delay the calculation of ROI.

KEY FINANCIAL TOOLS

Payback or Payout: A reasonable question for top management to ask is "how long will it take to get our money back?" The length of time to recover invested funds is frequently viewed as a measure of risk. From the product planner's standpoint, the period of time until the project begins to pay back is the period that the project is most vulnerable to competitive actions. So payback is a useful piece of information. The formula for calculating payback is quite simple:

$$\frac{\text{Investment}}{\text{Annual Net Cash Flow}} = \text{Payback}$$

Since cash flow tends to build period-to-period in new product development as the new product expands distribution and develops repeat business, a more practical method is to accumulate estimated cash flow period-by-period until the total equals the total investment. The length of time is expressed in months.

Break-even Analysis: The break-even point is the volume of sales at which the business will neither earn income nor incur a loss. It is the point at which expired costs, or expenses, and revenue are exactly equal. This tells the product planner how much latitude he has to be wrong about sales levels. Table 8 is a formula and an example.

Return on Investment: Eventually, you will almost surely have to calculate ROI. The formula looks like this:

$$\frac{\text{Sales}}{\text{Invested Capital}} \times \frac{\text{Net Income}}{\text{Sales}}$$

$$\frac{\text{Net Income}}{\text{Invested Capital}} = \text{ROI} \qquad \text{so}$$

```
Total variable expenses equal 60% of sales
Total fixed costs equal $120,000
Maximum sales volume at full capacity equals $600,000
Therefore:

        1.00BE  =  .60BE + $120,000
1.00BE − .60BE  =  $120,000
        .40BE   =  $120,000
           BE   =  $300,000

In this example, break-even occurs at about 50% of capacity.
```

Table 8. A sample break-even analysis

What is defined as invested capital has a major impact on the appearances of profitability. It is one thing to calculate ROI for an on-going business where the net income number is relatively definite. It is quite another to calculate it on a future project.

Figure 21 shows how one large company calculates new product ROI.

SPECIFYING "IF-THEN" RULES

If-then rules specify in advance when you should consider folding a project. Once a project gets into prototype development, it tends to take on a life of its own. It has acquired at least one strong backer in the organization. If it is at all interesting, it will acquire a momentum that will carry it past "warning lights."

Since you know right now that it is unlikely that every project that gets past screening is going to get to test market, your policy should be to set rules in advance to terminate each project if certain specified objectives are not met at certain specific points.

If-then rules are not set for every individual step. They should concentrate on the points where major amounts of time and/or money

NEW PRODUCT FINANCIAL ANALYSIS

COMPARATIVE RETURN ON INVESTMENT SUMMARY

($000)

Description of New Product_____

Date of Planned National Introduction_____

Planned Gross Selling Price_____

	Incremental Cost Basis					Full Absorption Basis		
	Develop & Test Market	National Introduction		1st Normal Year		1st Normal Year		Total Current Company Plan
	Amount	Amount	%	Amount	%	Amount	%	%
Time Span								
Case Sales Volume								
Gross Sales								

Sales Deductions
  Cash Discounts
  Transportation
  Promotions/
    Allowances
  Other Deductions								

Total Sales Deductions								
Net Sales								

Cost of Sales
  Incremental
  Indirect Burden								

Total Cost								
Gross Profit								

Operating Expenses
  Advertising
  Agency Expenses
  Non-variable
    Sales Promotion								

Figure 21. An ROI summary sheet for new product development

	Incremental Cost Basis					Full Absorption Basis		
	Develop & Test Market	National Introduction		1st Normal Year		1st Normal Year		Total Current Company Plan
	Amount	Amount	%	Amount	%	Amount	%	%
Time Span								
Selling Expenses								
Marketing Services Market Research Graphics Packaging								
Warehouse & Shipping								
Product & Process Technology								
G & A								
Operating & Engineering								
Other Expenses								
Total Operating Expenses								
Profit (Loss) From Operations								
Investment								
Fixed Assets								
Accumulated Depreciation								
Net Fixed Assets								
Accounts Receivable								
Inventory								
Total Investment								
Return on Net Assets								

Prepared by: _____   Date: _____

Figure 21. Continued

are required to take the project to the next step, e.g., from lab bench-top samples to pilot plant production. If-then rules should concentrate on the aspects of the new product that are crucial to its success in the market.

Some examples might be:

If the production costs on the retort pouch project do not meet conventional frozen food production costs within 18 months, or before $650,000 in R&D funds have been expended, *then* the project will be abandoned.

If engineering studies do not support 2,000 hours of trouble free performance from the electric sledge hammer by March 1, 198—, *then* the project will be terminated.

If the ultra high temperature asceptic processed flavored milk products cannot meet a six-month unrefrigerated shelf life standard within the budget of 450 man-hours of R&D time, *then* the project will be put on suspension until such time as a technical breakthrough is made somewhere else in the industry.

XI

Turning the New Product Process into Reality: Prototype Development

This Section addresses the work of turning an idea or concept into an actual product. The specific technical work that takes place in research and development (R&D) is beyond our interests here. What is of interest is the process by which R&D work is guided and directed as you develop new products.

The same process of setting objectives, designing a prototype, testing it, refining the prototype, testing it again, and repeating the process until a final version is achieved is common to both heavy industrial machinery and consumer packaged goods . What you must do is take the basic process and adapt it to your own requirements.

STUDYING THE R&D PROCESS

Before you begin to develop a system for working with R&D, consider two propositions. One, the evidence is quite convincing that most R&D departments are very good at what they do. You can expect to lose very few projects because the R&D people say "it can't be done." Relatively few new products fail because they are technical failures.

The other fact is that it is just as easy for R&D to develop the wrong product for you as it is for them to develop the right one. This is not to deny that there have been occasions when a lab breakthrough led to the development of an important new business. That does happen. But it is rare!

The point is that most R&D activity is purposeful and directed. A reasonable question follows—"why do so many unsuccessful products get to market?" There are two answers to that question. One is that R&D is given the wrong objectives to start. The other is that the objectives change along the way as the product is being developed.

Take an example of the wrong objectives. People use written documents to key punch cards which input data to the computer. Dozens of R&D departments were given the objective of eliminating the key punch step. They solved it with optical scanners.

After a decade and a half of explosive growth in data processing, optical scanning plays only a very minor role. The basic problem is that customers needed lower cost data handling systems, not higher cost systems.

The net result is that the prototype development system you set up in your company should 1) ensure that R&D is given the best possible initial objectives, and 2) make certain that your project review system continually focuses and re-focuses on those objectives.

SETTING OBJECTIVES

The fundamental working relationship between product planning and development people and R&D personnel should be kept straightforward. Product planners say what the new product *should do* and R&D decides *how it will do* that. Then the two parties negotiate their differences. We cannot overemphasize the importance of clear communications.

One of the best ways to establish such communications and maintain them throughout the life of the project is to prepare a *Product Development Objective Statement* for each project that you have in the

There is very little agreement on terminology in new product development, so it will be helpful to be specific about three particular words.

Concept: We use this term to refer to the idea for the new product and to the form of presenting the idea to customers. Concepts can be presented with words alone, or accompanied by illustrations.

Mock-up: This designates some *non-working* representation of the new product. It could be a drawing, a photograph, a dummy of the package, a scale model, etc. A mock-up gives the new product more definition than does a concept, but less than a prototype.

Prototype: A prototype is any *working* representation of the new product. A prototype can be developed to any level of completeness, until all of the decisions have been made. Then it becomes the final product.

Table 9. Some helpful definitions for prototype development

works. The objective statement should have at least eight specific sections. You may find that additional sections are useful in your business.

A convenient way to organize this material is in a looseleaf notebook. You can devote one page to each section and store supporting documents behind each section. The information in each section need not be extensive. A few sentences or paragraphs should be sufficient. If you can't condense the ideas in each section, it probably means that you're not clear on exactly what you are trying to do. The Planning Pages in Figure 23 at the end of this Section give you a practical basis on which to build your own product development objective statement.

An additional benefit from organizing your data in this manner is that it highlights what you *don't know* as well as what you do know. It highlights potential decisions, as well as decisions already reached.

Section One: The Original Concept Statement
The first section in your workbook (Planning Page 8) should be the original concept statement, the idea that the screening committee thought was worth pursuing. As the concept is exposed to more people

inside your organization, they will offer additional ideas and variations. These helpful new ideas are the first source of possible changes in your project. To the extent that these new suggestions logically fill out the concept, they are indeed helpful. Otherwise, they can distort what you are trying to accomplish. Placing the original concept in the first position in your workbook offers a source to keep reviewing to validate succeeding steps.

Section Two: Creative Strategy
The creative strategy statement (Planning Page 9) discussed in the Section on business analysis comes next. This highlights the *basic* benefit that the new product is expected to provide and tells how you expect to communicate this to prospective customers. The ability to communicate the benefit is just as important as the benefit itself.

Section Three: The Need to be Satisfied
The third segment (Planning Page 10) should describe the need that you believe exists among potential customers. This need that you expect to satisfy is the other side of the basic benefit in Section Two. It is useful to have a separate need statement to ensure that the project remains focused on the customers' requirements. The key question in negotiations with R&D is, "If we make this suggested alteration, what effect will it have on our ability to satisfy the customers' need?"

Section Four: A Description of the Prospective Customer
Another piece of information that will help to give R&D a clearer picture of its task is a description of the prospective customer (Planning Page 11). Examples might be:

> "All plants in SIC Code 381, Engineering and Scientific Instruments, with 100 employees or more, located East of the Mississippi River."

> "Current users of chewable antacid tablets, primarily the leading over-the-counter brands sold in drug stores and supermarkets."

"Men between the ages of 21 and 29, high school graduates with blue collar jobs, oriented towards active sports, who drink at least a case of beer a week."

Section Five: A Description of How the Product Will be Used

Even if it seems obvious, you should include a short statement (Planning Page 12) describing how you think the new product will be used by prospective customers. It is one more way to focus on the overall task and to help structure the development of the product.

Section Six: Target Costs

Your business analysis identified some intended selling price and some intended margin. To meet these targets, you must also meet a target cost. It is important to keep this target cost (Planning Page 13) in mind at all times because the great majority of the pressure in new product development tends to push costs up.

Section Seven: Extent of the Line

The number of varieties, styles, sizes, colors, flavors, etc. that you anticipate the new product will have should also be specified. Even if only one model is planned, state that (Planning Page 14).

Section Eight: Determinant Attributes

Every product has many attributes, or characteristics. But in most cases, only one or two determine whether the product will be purchased. It is very important to specify (Planning Page 15) what the determinant attributes of your new product will be. They establish the basis on which all other development trade-offs are made.

FOCUSING ON DETERMINANT ATTRIBUTES

Because every product has many attributes, it is easy to become sidetracked on interesting attributes, or elegant attributes, or high technology attributes. The Hoover Company, which makes vacuum cleaners, once developed a quiet vacuum cleaner. It focused its development efforts on the noise attribute of the machines. But that was not a determinant attribute. Quite the contrary, housewives equated noise with power, so a noiseless machine indicated lack of power. And power is a determinant attribute!

General Electric used an elegant technical solution to develop a light switch that didn't make noise. It was a flop in the market. It is important for people to hear and feel a click so that they can be confident that the lights are turned off.

In 1978, Amstar Corp., a major food products company, spent well over $1 million on advertising alone to introduce Domino Liquid Brown Sugar. By 1980, the product was struggling to hold on to its shelf space in supermarkets. Liquid Brown Sugar's major point of difference, it's major attribute, was that there were no lumps when you baked with the product. Unfortunately for Amstar, that was not a determinant attribute. The ability to use the product with existing recipes, however, was a determinant attribute. And cooks couldn't substitute Liquid Brown Sugar for regular refined brown sugar without changing recipes.

Sometimes a market is segmented in terms of determinant attributes. Toothpaste, for example, can do three things for consumers; it can prevent cavities, freshen breath and whiten teeth. These are also determinant attributes, *but* for different sets of customers in the market.

Sometimes one determinant attribute acts as a qualifier for another attribute. The determinant attributes in the market for fried snack food products like potato chips are freshness and flavor. Freshness is a "gate-keeper" attribute. If a new product does not deliver this attribute, flavor doesn't even get evaluated.

A fresh potato chip will break with a sharp snap. A stale chip will bend and eventually tear. Once a chip is judged fresh, the rest of the chip is eaten to determine the flavor. A stale chip is discarded without further evaluation.

The point of all this is that it is of the utmost importance that you understand what the determinant attributes are for your new product and that you keep developmental efforts focused directly on them. They are a key part of your product development objective statement.

IDENTIFYING DETERMINANT ATTRIBUTES

In most product categories, it is relatively easy to identify determinant attributes. They are the ones that people say are very important to them. Usually, a simple four point scale will identify them. Such a scale asks a question such as: "How important would you say _____ is to you? Would you say it is *very important, somewhat important, not too important* or *not at all important?"*

When doing research among customers on determinant attributes remember two things. One is that the statement of the attribute must be in terms that are relevant to the customer, not the manufacturer. For years, U.S. auto makers have asked American car buyers how important safety was to them. Customers have always said it was very important. Yet automobiles designed and marketed as safe cars always failed. Serious thinking should have led the auto makers to understand that virtually no one would purposely buy an unsafe car. The attribute, as stated, is simply not relevant.

The other point is that care should be taken to understand whether determinant attributes are segmenting a market, as is the case with toothpaste. If this is the case, it will most likely be seen in repeating patterns of attribute importance. Therefore, be particularly alert for patterns of importance. Run cross-tabulations of the data to see if the characteristics of the people who say *A* is very important are different from those who say *B* is very important.

TESTING AGAINST THE OBJECTIVES

As each new product development project goes forward, there is a repeating process of develop, test, and revise as the product moves closer and closer to some ideal format. A number of key points repeat themselves in new product development and require product developers and planners to make decisions about testing. It is worthwhile to examine some of the issues that product planners are faced with as the testing and retesting process goes on.

The kinds of testing that are of concern here are not the lab, or bench-top, tests that R&D is running for technical guidance. The testing of interest here involves obtaining evaluations from customers. That invariably means going outside your organization. A number of companies have excellent in-house sensory or product evaluation panels of employees which provide product development guidance outside a strictly laboratory testing environment.

These RGP's (Research Guidance Panels), as they are sometimes called, are well covered in technical literature. One good example is *Manual on Sensory Testing Methods*, published by the American Society for Testing and Materials, 1916 Race Street, Philadelphia, Pennsylvania, USA, 19103.

The testing problems and decisions that face product planners arise when R&D offers several alternative methods of proceeding. Or when R&D says, "Here, we've got what you asked for." At those times, there are just two alternatives. Make a judgment on your own, or test with customers. Remember that the majority of new products that fail do so because they don't fill a need in the marketplace. That doesn't mean that you never trust your own judgment. But it does mean that you should be very cautious about doing so.

TESTING MOCK-UPS AND PROTOTYPES

There are two basic kinds of information that you want to get from testing. One is predictive: Does this product form really meet the customers' needs and will it sell in the market? The second is diagnostic. How can we make this product better and what is wrong with the way it is now? The value of these data will vary depending on what you are testing and when in the development process you are testing.

This becomes clearer if you examine the essential elements of the testing process. The testing you are interested in is stimulus-response testing. Some stimulus—a concept, mock-up or prototype—is exposed to a group of customers and some response is elicited—reactions, evaluations, intentions.

The stimulus and responses that you are working with are surrogates for the real final product. The fact that they are different from the final product can be a significant source of error and/or reduced value of the data. Therefore, you must evaluate each testing situation in terms of the stimulus and response reality versus the desired information versus the cost of obtaining the information. As you make that evaluation, you should consider three major areas.

1. *Completeness of the stimulus:* A concept is a very incomplete stimulus. Many details are missing and the respondents who evaluate the stimuli must imagine the details for themselves. They are most likely to imagine details that they would prefer, although sometimes they may imagine problems. The most troublesome aspect is that each respondent in the test is probably imagining different details. As you move through the development process, you are filling in the details and making the stimuli increasingly complete, and most importantly, increasingly accurate.

The result is that, early in the developmental process, the diagnostic information is likely to be better than the predictive information. As you move through the developmental process, a shift takes place and the predictive data get better and the diagnostic data less valuable. You should have a clear understanding of the nature of the information that you are attempting to obtain and make your evaluation in terms of whether the stimuli are complete enough to elicit the type of response you need.

2. *The timing of the response:* One of the key response items is the answer to, "Would you buy this product if it were available?" The closer in real time that the respondent is to actually being able to make that decision on the market, the more accurate you can expect the response to be. Conversely, if you are testing two years before you can actually get to market, you cannot expect the same kind of accuracy. Where you are in your project timetable is important to your evaluation of the value of testing.

3. *The reality of the stimulus-response environment:* The question here is how close to reality are the conditions under which you will be testing. Actual purchases involve more than just the product itself. Pricing, distribution and myriad other factors affect the actual decision to buy, or not to buy. Until you actually get into test marketing, you

can't provide a completely real environment for your tests, but you can always be aware of the distortions that a lack of reality in the testing environment can create.

TESTING RECOMMENDATIONS

Always test with heavy users of the product category, or if no category exists, with respondents who are most favorably inclined toward the concept. This is particularly true when your primary interest is in diagnostic information.

The reasons for testing with heavy users are straightforward. In virtually every product category, a relatively small group of customers accounts for the majority of the volume. In general, you can expect about 20 percent of all your customers to account for about 80 percent of your total new product sales. Therefore, it is very important that you design a product that appeals strongly to this group.

Secondly, research has shown quite clearly that heavy users of a product category are *extremely more likely* to be *early* purchasers of a new product. So you want the help of this group to get sales momentum as quickly as possible.

Always test alternatives. There are two reasons for this rule. First, customers always have some choice in the marketplace, and offering alternatives provides additional realism. Even if there is no directly comparable product on the market, the customer always has the option of not using your new product and continuing to buy whatever he usually buys.

The second reason is that the test results from alternatives are very helpful in interpreting the results from the product you are testing. Everything is relative to something else. Test results do not offer much guidance as absolutes. The question is "Compared to what?"

Always test the product and the communications. At each step of the development process, you are trying to answer a series of questions. Does the product meet the need? Can we communicate that ability? Does the product match the communications?

Unless you develop your communications to the market along with your product, you risk not being able to communicate accurately with potential customers when the time comes to go to test market. You should involve your advertising department or advertising agency in the new product development project at a very early stage. If you give them limited assignments in developing communications, you can increase their involvement as the project becomes more and more detailed.

DEVELOPMENTAL TESTING METHODS

There are many methods for presenting mock-ups and prototypes to customers for evaluation during the developmental process. The limitations are set by the imaginations of the marketing research and product planning people, and the physical reality of the product itself.

Focus group interviews are widely used to evaluate mock-ups and prototypes during the development process. Such interviews tend to be expensive on a per respondent cost basis. But real opportunities for very valuable diagnostic information develop from the ability of a group of potential customers to interact while evaluating a prototype.

Focus group interviews do have limitations, and high technology products are one example. American Telephone & Telegraph Company, the Parsippany, New Jersey communications firm, believes that more customer involvement is necessary in developing high tech products. In order to guide its development efforts on a new visual communications terminal for deaf and hearing-impaired individuals, AT&T built a series of working models with different sized keyboards, screens and other important features. They then invited a panel of deaf and hearing-impaired consumers to a test facility where the models were available for inspection and evaluation. The company made important design feature decisions based on the data developed in this test.

To guide its development of a home electronic information system, where both hardware and software are important, AT&T built some working models and placed them in the homes of respondents. In this way, they put together a panel of customers to provide evaluative feedback on a wide variety of questions as the project developed.

One major manufacturer of heavy earth moving equipment

built scale models of its proposed new products. These scale models were displayed in an appropriately constructed sand box at the annual industry trade show. Selected potential customers were invited to use the models. Their subsequent opinions and comments provided valuable product development guidance.

ONE COMPANY'S "ADVISORY PANELS"

Moray Industries Ltd. is a small company headquartered in Devonport, Auckland, New Zealand. Moray designs and manufactures wet suits, jackets and other accessories made of various types of foamed rubber. These products are used in scuba diving, surfing, sailing and, most recently, wind surfing. Moray must compete with major companies in New Zealand and with imports from even larger companies in Australia and the United States. Moray has carved a niche for itself in the market by using its size to advantage by beating everyone else to the market with new ideas.

Moray has recruited "Advisory Panels" to help them evaluate the steady stream of new ideas that are required to stay ahead. Each sport or end market has a separate panel. Moray asked each of its major retail customers in the Auckland area to nominate one surfer, etc., from among the store's customers to serve on the Moray Advisory Panel (which was also good for trade relations).

After screening, each member is presented with a jacket identifying him/her as a member of the Moray Advisory Panel. Since these jackets are worn by very popular young men and young women at the places where the sport takes place, there is an additional public relations advantage. The real payoff, however, is in the luncheon meetings which advisory panel members attend for a very nominal fee. At these meetings, a wide variety of new product ideas are exposed and evaluated. Concept boards, mock-ups, and prototypes are used as stimuli. Since most of the products are easily fabricated, prototypes can be made for individual panel members for actual in-use testing. Moray has crafted an exceptionally flexible and useful testing program for out-of-pocket expenses of less than NZ$2,000 annually.

IN-USE TESTING

Toward the end of the development phase, many companies give serious consideration to a large-scale in-use test. In this final test before test marketing, a random sample of potential customers is selected from a known universe and asked to use a sample of the product for a certain period of time. The primary purpose of such testing is predictive.

This testing is expensive and time-consuming. Not every product can actually be in-use tested. Think of the logistics involved in a test of 250 randomly selected households testing living room sofas. In any case, there are still a great number of products that can be tested in in-use situations.

Skipping in-use testing when it is possible is an extremely poor use of resources. In-use testing is the last step before test marketing and test marketing almost always requires an investment much larger than all of the developmental funds expended prior to it. The companies with the best success records rarely, if ever, skip in-use testing.

DIMENSIONS IN SAMPLING

One of the first questions you'll have to deal with in in-use testing is sample size since it is the primary determinant of the budget required. Selecting an appropriate sample size involves making a trade-off between accuracy (acceptable level of risk) and cost. Drawing a sample from some larger population always includes the possibility of error, that is, the sample you draw won't actually match the total population. There are, however, quite specific mathematical rules that describe the relationship between error and sample size.

We will not treat the statistics of sampling in detail here, but an overview will be helpful. Accuracy (or potential for error) is a function of sample size and the true nature of the condition in the total population that you are trying to measure.

The "traditional" bag of black and white marbles is a good way to illustrate these principles. Imagine a bag in which 90 percent of the marbles are black and 10 percent are white. It doesn't matter how big the bag is. If you randomly selected 10 marbles from the bag, you could get nine black ones and one white one, i.e., a true reflection of the contents.

But you could also get other combinations, say five white and five black. or perhaps all black. In any of these events, you would make a bad judgment about the true state of events.

If instead you drew a sample of 100 marbles, you could get exactly 90 black ones and 10 white ones, but you might also get 89 black and 11 white, or 85 black and 15 white, or 92 black and 8 white. In any of these outcomes, you would be much better prepared to estimate the conditions than you were with the sample of 10.

If you drew a sample of 1,000 marbles your chances of being wrong are even less. At each sample size, you can calculate the chances of being wrong precisely. The problem is that the relationship between sample size and error is not linear. That is, when you double the sample size, you don't double your chances of being right, you only increase them about 50 percent. So increasing sample size may be an effective way to deal with risk, but it is not a very efficient one.

OTHER DIMENSIONS IN SAMPLING

The other part of the equation is the actual nature of the total population. Change the proportion of marbles in the bag so that now 51 percent are black and 49 percent are white. Your task remains the same, to decide whether the bag has more black or white marbles. As you can quickly tell, your sample of 1,000 marbles is much more likely to give the right answer than is a sample of 10, or even 100. And a sample of 10,000 would be even better.

This is the way in which sample size and the true state of conditions in the total population interact to determine error. There is one further dimension to this problem. That is the question of getting the right answer when you draw just *one* sample.

If you drew 10 samples from the bag above, some might have 52 black and 48 white, others might have 50 black and 50 white and so on. But, if you average all of the samples, you'd have a better chance of estimating 51 black and 49 white than if you drew just one sample. This problem is dealt with by the notion of standard deviation.

Standard deviations specify the odds that you could get the sample results you got solely by chance, and not because of the true state of events. Market researchers usually deal with three levels of standard deviation. At one standard deviation, the chances are one out of three that your results could be due completely to chance. At two standard deviations, they fall to five out of 100. At three standard deviations, odds fall to one out of 100 that your results could be accidental. The problem is that calculating standard deviations treats repeated samples similarly to larger sample sizes.

Therefore, to improve your odds without taking repeated samples, you have to increase the sample size. Thus, all three dimensions interact to define the risk level at any particular sample size. Fortunately, most researchers and executives agree that the odds at one standard deviation are too great to accept, and the odds at three standard deviations are too expensive to achieve in most new product development work. Therefore, the norm is widely accepted as two standard deviations which produces the chances that 95 times out of 100, you will be right.

Figure 22 shows the relationship between various sample sizes and the true state of events. The numbers in the table define the range of results you could get 95 times out of 100 at that sample size and that state of events.

For example, the intersection of sample size 250 and the state of the total population, 6 percent or 94 percent, reads 3.0. This means that if that sample size and that proportion were the actual state of affairs, you could expect to get results between 97 percent and 91 percent 95 times out of 100. (Or conversely, results between 3 percent and 9 percent.)

FIVE CRUCIAL POINTS IN PROTOTYPE DEVELOPMENT

Experience has demonstrated that there are five points that are easy to forget in the actual development process, and forgetting them always leads to trouble.

1. Insist that the primary point of all testing activities be to ensure that the prototype matches the concept. It is possible that focus

ERROR RANGE AT TWO STANDARD DEVIATIONS
(95 out of 100 odds)

The Actual State of Events in the Total Population Is:

SAMPLE SIZE	2% or 98%	4% or 96%	6% or 94%	10% or 90%	15% or 85%	20% or 80%	25% or 75%	30% or 70%	35% or 65%	40% or 60%	45% or 55%	50%
					Range of Error (in Percent Plus or Minus)							
25	5.6	7.8	9.5	12.0	14.3	16.0	17.3	18.3	19.1	19.6	19.8	20.0
50	4.0	5.6	6.8	8.5	10.1	11.4	12.3	13.0	13.5	13.9	14.1	14.2
75	3.2	4.5	5.5	6.9	8.2	9.2	10.0	10.5	11.0	11.3	11.4	11.5
100	2.8	3.9	4.8	6.0	7.1	8.0	8.7	9.2	9.5	9.8	9.9	10.0
150	2.3	3.2	3.9	4.9	5.9	6.6	7.1	7.5	7.8	8.0	8.1	8.2
200	2.0	2.8	3.4	4.3	5.1	5.7	6.1	6.5	6.8	7.0	7.0	7.1
250	1.8	2.5	3.0	3.8	4.5	5.0	5.5	5.8	6.0	6.2	6.2	6.3
300	1.6	2.3	2.8	3.5	4.1	4.6	5.0	5.3	5.5	5.7	5.8	5.8
400	1.4	2.0	2.4	3.0	3.6	4.0	4.3	4.6	4.8	4.9	5.0	5.0
500	1.3	1.8	2.1	2.7	3.2	3.6	3.9	4.1	4.3	4.4	4.5	4.5
600	1.1	1.6	2.0	2.5	2.9	3.3	3.6	3.8	3.9	4.0	4.1	4.1
800	.98	1.4	1.7	2.1	2.5	2.8	3.0	3.2	3.3	3.4	3.5	3.5
1000	.90	1.3	1.5	1.9	2.3	2.6	2.8	2.9	3.1	3.1	3.2	3.2
1200	.81	1.1	1.4	1.7	2.1	2.3	2.5	2.7	2.8	2.8	2.9	2.9
1500	.73	1.0	1.2	1.6	1.9	2.1	2.3	2.4	2.5	2.5	2.6	2.6
2000	.61	.86	1.0	1.3	1.6	1.8	1.9	2.0	2.1	2.2	2.2	2.2
2500	.56	.78	.95	1.2	1.4	1.6	1.7	1.8	1.9	2.0	2.0	2.0
3000	.51	.71	.87	1.1	1.3	1.5	1.6	1.7	1.7	1.8	1.8	1.8
4000	.44	.62	.75	.95	1.1	1.3	1.4	1.4	1.5	1.5	1.6	1.6

Figure 22. The relationship among various sample sizes at two standard deviations

of attention can shift to the prototype because it is tangible and the concept is intangible.

In fact, it is possible that during prototype development, you may come up with a terrific idea for a *different* new product from the one you're working on. That's fine, but make sure that it becomes a *different* development project.

2. If customers aren't users or potential users of the new product, they are of no interest to you. The time and money pressures in new product development lead to temptations to take short-cuts in testing. One of the worst short-cuts to take is to use "convenience" samples of customers, that is respondents whose sole qualifications are that they are handy and willing to cooperate. Always keep your eye on the heavy users.

3. If the respondents in your test do not *believe* that a product characteristic is a benefit to them, then it *is not* a benefit, no matter how much you and R&D would like to think otherwise. The temptation is to concentrate on what is easiest to do, the characteristics that you are most certain you can deliver. This can also occur in situations where you cannot communicate the benefit in a believable way. That is the reason that your communications should always be developed and tested parallel to the prototype.

4. If a benefit is not *important* to the customer, then it *isn't important* to you. This is the question of ensuring that you have identified the determinant attributes of the product category and are concentrating on improving them.

5. If customers do not believe that you *deliver* the promised benefit, then you *don't deliver* it. It is the difference between lab testing and real world testing. It is the difference between what *you* think your advertising says and what *customers* think it says.

THE FINAL STEPS IN PROTOTYPE DEVELOPMENT

The focus of the *previous* material was on four crucial aspects of the new product development process:

1. The market
2. The physical product
3. The financial numbers
4. The communications to the market

In focusing on just these four topics, a whole range of other aspects of the development process has been ignored. Those aspects are important, but secondary. They also tend to divert attention from the hard decisions about the four crucial aspects.

Some of the secondary aspects of the new product development you should do concurrently with prototype and communications development:

- Write raw materials specifications
- Develop production specifications

- Prepare handling, warehousing and shipping policies
- Select product name
- Develop full pricing package (discounts, terms, etc.)
- Fulfill legal requirements
- Create advertising
- Develop sales promotion material and salesmen's materials
- Determine packaging and labelling
- Specify sales training programs
- Define trade programs
- Coordinate sales reporting, control and feedback systems
- Specify pilot plant production quantities
- Select test market(s)
- Anticipate competitive reaction
- Identify key accounts.

This list is not exhaustive, nor is every item on it appropriate for every company. It suggests additional activities that will accompany the development of the four crucial aspects of developing a new product.

Also, the kinds of items on the list above are much closer to your normal everyday business activities, which means that you have experience dealing with them. Thus, they involve less risk. Remember that they are important, but not crucial. If you allow them to become crucial, you will put your project into great jeopardy.

BEWARE RUSHING THE PROCESS

There will be a lot of pressure to get your new products to market as quickly as possible. Top management wants to see results from its investment; there is a desire to beat the competition; there is the personal satisfaction for the development people in seeing their work move out of the lab and into the market. A project should move along at a brisk pace because time really is money. Also, winning projects seem to have a momentum of their own, and if they lose that momentum, they are likely to falter.

But, all of these pressures should not lead you to introduce a product into the market until the product is really ready. The danger words are, "We'll take care of that later."

When IBM introduced a new generation of computers in 1979, it put significant presure on all its competitors. Burroughs Corp., the Detroit computer manufacturer, responded by introducing five new computer systems during 1979 and 1980. The Burrough's concepts were excellent, but the actual products couldn't deliver the promises of the concepts. While it is difficult to know exactly how much this hurry-up introduction contributed to Burrough's sharply declining 1980 and 1981 earnings, there is no doubt it did contribute.

PRODUCT DEVELOPMENT OBJECTIVE STATEMENT

Section One
Original Concept Statement

Statement of the problem to be solved. Description of the need that exists:

_____

_____

_____

_____

Description of the solution that this product will supply:

_____

_____

_____

_____

Attributes of the new product that will make this solution possible:

_____

_____

_____

_____

Figure 23. Your own product development objective statement

Product Planning Page 9

PRODUCT DEVELOPMENT OBJECTIVE STATEMENT

Section Two
Creative Strategy

Principal benefit offered by the new product:

_____

_____

_____

_____

Reason why this benefit is possible:

_____

_____

_____

_____

Product character/Personality:

_____

_____

_____

_____

Figure 23. Continued

What the product is/What it is used for:

_____

_____

_____

_____

Figure 23. Continued

PRODUCT DEVELOPMENT OBJECTIVE STATEMENT

Section Three
Need to Be Satisfied

Description of customer's need/problem:

_____

_____

_____

_____

_____

Special circumstances, if any, affecting the need/problem:

_____

_____

_____

_____

Source of data:

_____

_____

Figure 23. Continued

PRODUCT DEVELOPMENT OBJECTIVE STATEMENT

Section Four .
Description of Prospective Customer

_____

_____

_____

_____

_____

_____

How often will customer use product:

_____

_____

How much of the product will customer use each time:

_____

_____

Source of data:

_____

_____

Figure 23. Continued

PRODUCT DEVELOPMENT OBJECTIVE STATEMENT

Section Five
Description of How Product Will Be Used

_____

_____

_____

_____

_____

Special circumstances, if any, affecting product use:

_____

_____

Directly competitive products:

_____

_____

Indirectly competitive products:

_____

_____

Source of data:

_____

Figure 23. Continued

PRODUCT DEVELOPMENT OBJECTIVE STATEMENT

Section Six
Target Costs:

Suggested retail selling price:

Size/Pack planned:

Retailer's percentage margin:

Customary retailer margins on similar products:

Price to retailer:

Distributor's percentage margin:

Customary retailer margins on similar products:

Price to distributor:

Figure 23. Continued

Manufacturer's selling price:

_____

Cost of goods:

_____

Gross margin:

_____

Selling expenses:

_____

Other expenses:

_____

Net profit:

_____

Figure 23. Continued

PRODUCT PLANNING OBJECTIVE STATEMENT

Section Seven
Number of Items In The Line

Description of line items at introduction:

_____

_____

_____

_____

_____

Description of items that could be added to the line later:

_____

_____

_____

_____

_____

_____

Figure 23. Continued

PRODUCT DEVELOPMENT OBJECTIVE STATEMENT

Section Eight
Determinant Attributes

Most important attributes:

_____

_____

_____

Second most important attributes:

_____

_____

_____

Third most important attributes:

_____

_____

Does any attribute act as a gatekeeper? Describe:

_____

_____

_____

Figure 23. Continued

List other important attributes:

_____

_____

Source of data:

_____

_____

Figure 23. Continued

XII

The Final Step: The Commercialization of Your Product

Up to this point in the new product development process, no customer has actually paid money to obtain one of the products under development. When you are ready to start selling your product, you have reached the final stage.

The sales activity may take place in a limited, controlled environment, or it may be on a national level, or on some in-between basis. Exactly how you decide to begin to sell your new product is a *very* important decision because it almost always represents a significant financial commitment.

The basic decision at this juncture is to either "freeze" development and introduce the product as it stands, or to continue development through a variety of sales testing situations. That is, the choice is a widespread introduction or more testing. The number of factors to be considered require careful analysis and a decision that balances risk and cost.

ANALYZING PRODUCTION COSTS

The first consideration is production costs. Airplanes are never sold in test situations because the cost of production of the first unit is so high. But, major aircraft manufacturers work closely with their potential customers from the concept stage onward. They begin to minimize risk as early as possible in the development process.

Automobile manufacturers don't test market their new products for the same reason. However they do a substantial amount of customer research as prototypes are being developed. They do attempt to minimize risk during the development phase.

Numerous products have initial production costs that are so large as to prohibit any form of sales testing. But, as you move down the production cost ladder, the alternatives become less absolute. Manufacturers of consumer durables seldom market test their products for essentially the same reasons that automobile manufacturers do not, i.e., production costs. Some claim it would require tooling and other production expenses in the range of $1 million to $3 million to obtain test merchandise, and what could be learned from additional sales testing is not worth the expense.

They further argue that retailer support and the efforts of floor sales people are extremely important factors in the success of new washing machines, TV sets, trash compactors, etc. There is no acceptable way to test these influences.

ADDRESSING THE QUESTION OF SECRECY

Another consideration is the question of secrecy. When you take your new product into any in-market sales testing, competitors get a chance to look at the product, and possibly copy it. Therefore, the question of secrecy does deserve consideration.

Generally, the question of secrecy is vastly overrated. Competitors are given too much credit for their ability to analyze the market and come to the same conclusions that you did.

There are some industries where secrecy is truly important. In the women's fashion business, new designs are never tested because it is easy to make copies quickly.

The final point about secrecy is that if your competitors can beat you to the market if you test your product, then it is not likely to be a very expensive market to enter. Accordingly, your financial exposure is most likely modest and it may be more appropriate to skip testing.

DECIDING WHETHER OR NOT TO TEST

The point of market testing your new product is two-fold—to continue to fine-tune the development of your complete offering and to gain some assurance that your volume estimates are reasonable. Therefore, the objective of testing is to minimize the risk that you have overlooked some major problem that could prevent you from executing your plans and reaching your goals.

Testing reduces risk and such risk reduction has a price. The decision of whether or not to test involves an assessment of the amount of risk inherent in the project, an estimate of the costs required to reduce that risk, and an evaluation of the best trade-off between the two.

In making that evaluation, there are three factors that you should first consider.

1. What is the probability of success without testing and how much additional profit would be generated by a national introduction compared to the costs of a failure? While testing can minimize risk, it cannot maximize profits, so this is a good place to begin the analysis. There are times when the risks are low and expenses modest, and a direct national introduction makes good sense. That usually involves items such as line-extensions of your existing products which represent markets and customers that you know very well. They also usually represent only minor profit opportunities so the costs of testing would be disproportionate.

2. Can the test situation be supplied with a pilot plant? Ideally, you would like to limit your manufacturing investment until you can be reasonably certain your product will be successful. If you can't operate out of a pilot plant and must make a major plant investment, the difference in costs between testing and not test-

ing will be sharply altered. In those circumstances, the additional profits from a national introduction become more attractive.

3. What demands will a national introduction make on your marketing resources? A national introduction that requires a heavy investment in advertising and inventory makes testing a more attractive proposition. In particular, how heavy will the demands be on your sales force in a national introduction? If the new product requires that a lot of time be diverted from your existing business, testing may be the better decision.

ADDITIONAL CONSIDERATIONS FOR INDUSTRIAL PRODUCTS

Manufacturers of industrial products are more likely to skip testing than consumer products manufacturers. Industrial products companies believe that they are closer to their markets and know their customers better than consumer products companies. To a certain degree, that is true. But industrial product markets have requirements that can be missed by being "too close."

WHAT TO TEST

By the time your new product project has reached this point, it is virtually certain that one or more critical assumptions on which the success of the project hinges will have evolved. Your testing should focus on two things. One point of focus is the critical assumption and the other is the total package you are bringing to market.

Another way to look at this question is to return to your version of the "Build-Up Estimating Model" discussed in Section IX. This model is a representation of what you expect your business to look like. One testing goal is to see how all the parts of this system work together in actual practice. The other is to check the critical assumptions that lie inside each of the components in Table 7.

For instance, a critical assumption might be that you can

One major study of industrial new product failures uncovered six problem areas that are unique to industrial products. A careful review of how much much you actually know about these six areas should be a part of your decision to test, or not to test.

1. The lack of a really precise definition of the segment of the total market which will place the greatest value on your new product. One example would be defining the market as industrial contract air conditioning firms, when the high value segment is really industrial contract air conditioning firms *specializing in large scale computer installations.*

2. Underestimating the level of marketing effort actually required to achieve volume targets. It is easy to convince yourself that your new product is so sensational that it will be bought on the first sales call, maybe the second at worst. In fact, it may take six calls spread over a full year. The impact that such a difference could have on your production and financial planning is major.

3. Failing to fully understand the level of new investment that a potential customer will have to make to take full advantage of the benefits your new product offers. Or failing to fully appreciate the extent to which your new product will make obsolete the customer's production processes.

4. Failing to fully appreciate the demands that the new products will make on the customers' technical and application skills. The food that you ate on your last airlines flight is a good example. Dozens of food products companies could supply markedly better meals, and most airline food service managers would prefer them. The problem is that cabin personnel refuse to supply the additional effort at the point of serving that would make the difference.

5. Incomplete understanding of purchasing processes and the serious underestimating of the time required to gain trial purchases. In rapidly growing, high technology fields, it is often quite difficult to identify who actually influences purchase decisions.

6. Failing to fully appreciate the existing relationships and influence patterns among prospective customers and their existing vendors. Past favors done are invisible to the outsider, but can be very powerful factors in preventing vendor changes. This is particularly true in older, established slow-growth markets.

achieve a given level of trial purchasing. That indicates a critical question is your ability to communicate the principal benefit in a meaningful, action-inducing fashion. Or, it might be repeat purchases which translates to "does the product deliver the promised benefit?" Or, it might be demand at the proposed price level. The point is that it may be important to you to be able to test alternative versions of critical assumptions, say two different advertising approaches or two different price levels.

If testing critical assumptions, and especially alternative versions of those assumptions, is important to you, there are testing procedures where customers buy the new product, but do so under limited conditions. These testing methods fit between full scale in-use tests and test marketing.

SALES WAVE TESTING

Sales wave tests are the most artificial of the three major methods because the fewest elements of an actual market place environment are present. But sales wave tests do give you a very large amount of control over the situation. Therefore, they offer an opportunity to test a variety of alternatives.

Sales wave tests generally begin with identification of a sample of prospective customers. Then each prospective customer is shown some example of the planned marketing communication, frequently a proposed advertisement. The prospective customer is offered a free sample of the product. Then, at the anticipated repurchase interval, the prospective customers are re-contacted and offered the opportunity to buy more of the product. This re-contacting and repeat purchasing can take as many waves as are necessary to validate the assumptions being tested.

Contacts can be made via telephone and repeat purchases delivered by mail or parcel delivery service. Or a route may be set up much like a milkman's route, and deliveries made right off the route truck. Interviews with the customers can take place at any appropriate times during the test period.

SIMULATED STORE TESTING

In this method of testing, prospective customers are invited to visit a simulated store, some obviously limited version of the type of retail outlet in which the new product would eventually be sold. Again, the prospective customer is usually shown some advertising for the new product, and probably for competitors as well. The customer is then given some modest money amount ($2 to $5) to spend on merchandise displayed in the simulated store.

It is then possible to invite the customers back for repeat visits, or to re-contact them as is done in sales wave testing. The advantage that simulated store testing has over sales wave testing is that competitive products and competitive communications can also be included in the decision structure.

CONTROLLED STORE TESTING

This method of testing can be looked at as "mini-test marketing." A sample of actual retail outlets in one or more markets is recruited and the product is offered for sale exactly as you would expect it to be in full test marketing.

Obviously, this method is the most "lifelike" and least artificial of the three. But it still provides considerable ability to test price levels, package designs, etc. Controlled store testing, however, removes you the farthest from the individual customer.

The descriptions of these three methods are only general and there is wide latitude for inventive variations. For example, Tetsudo Kosaikai is the 10th largest sales organization in Japan. The company operates 4,000 kiosk stores throughout Japan. Some manufacturers use these kiosks quite successfully to conduct controlled store tests.

HOW TO GET LIMITED TESTING DONE

Any competent, experienced marketing research organization should be able to plan and conduct sales wave testing. You should be able to design such tests with your regular supplier. If not, get recommendations from other people in your industry.

Simulated store testing is a more specialized type of research and is most often done by marketing research firms that concentrate on such testing. Assign your regular marketing research supplier to the task of evaluating and recommending the firms available for this type of research. In many cities, the facilities for simulated store testing may not exist and will have to be developed.

Controlled store testing is also conducted by a number of marketing research firms. The world's largest marketing research organization, the A. C. Nielsen Company, calls its controlled store testing service in the U.S. *Data Markets.* It provides a complete package of

---

Overseas, A. C. Nielsen also offers these services:

Belgium	As many as 24 supermarkets.
France	A large choice of supermarkets for use in matched panel testing, in Latin Square test designs and in side-by-side tests.
West Germany	The Nordhessen has been set up as a special area for testing in supermarkets.
Netherlands	Controlled store tests are available in a variety of types of retail outlets.
Spain	Controlled store testing is available in Madrid and Barcelona.
Sweden	A panel of two sets of 20 food stores (excludes co-op and department stores) is available in the Great Gothenburg area for test purposes.
Switzerland	Controlled store testing is available in a variety of stores in different cities.
United Kingdom	Panels of matched large volume self-service stores are available for controlled store testing.
Australia	Controlled store testing is available for food stores, chemists and confectionery outlets.
New Zealand	Controlled store tests are arranged upon request.
Austria	Controlled store tests are conducted in 24 large self-service stores in the Vienna area.
Canada	Panels of large chain stores are available for a wide variety of controlled store testing situations.

---

warehousing, stocking, auditing, sales and reporting services. For information, write International Headquarters, Nielsen Plaza, Northbrook, IL, U.S.A.60062. (See Appendix).

Success in setting up your own controlled store testing environment may very well depend on engaging the services of a competent research firm since considerable attention to detail is required. Particular attention must be paid to maintaining inventories because an out-of-stock situation that is not known to you can seriously distort the results of the test.

CONDUCTING TEST MARKETING

Test marketing generally takes place when you sell your new product through normal trade channels in one or more selected geographic areas where you use all of the marketing tools that you would expect to use on a national level. Some countries, however, are too small to provide a selection of representative markets. In others it is impossible to simulate national advertising. In those cases, test marketing assumes the character of the beginning of a national roll-out.

Again, the objective of test marketing is the market evaluation of your total program and the accuracy of your critical assumptions. The key questions to be answered in test marketing are 1) Are we hitting our volume targets? and 2) Can we improve our program in any way? Data collection in test marketing concentrates on customer response, trade response and competitive response. Some major points are:

Customer Response:

- Level of awareness
- Market penetration/rate of trial purchasing
- Repeat purchasing (where appropriate)
- Source of knowledge about new product
- Performance expectations
- Who is actually buying the product
- How customer buying patterns have changed
- Apparent price sensitivity

- Image projected by the product and the advertising
- Reactions to marketing communications

Trade Response:

- Extent of distribution
- Apparent level of support
- Re-ordering patterns
- Actual display patterns
- How product is warehoused and handled
- Trade attitudes
- Trade commitment

Competitive Response:

- Pricing changes
- Promotion spending level changes
- Advertising/selling message content changes
- Sales force behavior changes

PLANNING FOR TEST MARKETING

Test marketing requires very careful, thoughtful and detailed planning. You are asking potential customers, your distributors and your own organization to do something that they have never done before. You are asking them to change behavior patterns. Accomplishing such behavior changes requires a high level of coordination among all parties.

Test marketing planning begins with the format that you use for marketing planning for your existing products. This provides an important point of reference for other people in your organization.

Your regular marketing planning, however, will most likely be inadequate for test marketing planning because it will not be detailed enough in certain crucial areas. Regular marketing planning builds on experience and knowledge that is missing in a new product introduction. Pricing, sales presentations, distribution and promotion are the areas of planning that need extra levels of effort and detail in new product marketing planning.

It is imporant to point out that all of this discussion of test marketing planning is equally applicable to planning for a national introduction. All the fundamental problems exist in either situation. In a national introduction, the cost of overlooking one of those problems is far greater. So detailed planning is even more important in a national introduction.

PRICING PLANNING

The Build-Up Estimating Model shown in Section X treated costs and prices as *"givens,"* but this is not necessarily so. The Model assumes the most widely used method of establishing prices, i.e., the production department provides an estimate of the cost of goods to which an estimate of marketing expenses is added. A further addition is made to include the desired level of profitability. In this method, a price is literally "forced" out and seldom receives much further analysis.

The key point is that this method treats costs as fixed. Doing so sharply limits the planning options available to new product development people. There is a substantial body of evidence that this treatment of costs is unnecessarily simplistic. Rather than remain fixed, costs come down at some regular rate with each doubling of production. This behavior is usually known as the "experience effect."

If your cost structure has the possibility of displaying an experience effect, you have additional pricing possibilities. Texas Instruments (TI) Inc. used the anticipated experience effect in producing hand-held calculators to price its initial products below initial costs when it entered that market. Those lower prices caused a rapid expansion in the market and great hardship among Texas Instruments competitors. TI ended up dominating the product category. It did exactly the same thing when it entered the digital wrist watch market, with exactly the same results.

The first models of SONY Inc.'s personal portable stereo radio player, WALKMAN, had a cost structure that would have required a retail price of about $217. Instead of simply following the build-up pricing method, SONY targeted a retail price of $143 and relied on the

Pathmark is a major U.S. supermarket chain. It uses eight key criteria in deciding whether to buy a new item. Those criteria are:

1. *Advertising support*

   Pathmark is exceptionally interested in the amount of money that the manufacturer is planning to spend to "sell-through" the new product. Multi-media campaigns and coupons are important points. The amount of money to be spent is evaluated in relation to the total amount spent in the product category.

2. *Product Uniqueness*

   A truly new product is the type of item that excites Pathmark because it brings "new" sales since it satisfies an untapped demand. This creates long-term sales growth and puts new dollars into the cash registers.

3. *Introductory Allowances*

   The allowance must be deep enough to make it worthwhile for Pathmark to discontinue some other item.

4. *Profitability*

   Does the profitability of the new item at least match the gross profit in the product category? If the new item is bought, can it increase the overall profit mix?

Figure 24. A supermarket chain's key criteria for buying new products

experience effect to drive costs down with large volume production. SONY's worldwide sales of WALKMAN are estimated at about 3,500,000 units.

Careful examination of the nature of your anticipated costs, along with estimates of total sales volumes at differing price levels, should be an integral part of your planning. This does not mean that a significant experience effect is possible in every industry. In mature industries, the chances of improving production technology are relatively few and the length of time required for a doubling of production can be so long that experience effects are of little practical value to the product planner.

5. *Test Market Results*
   Does the manufacturer have test market results that show what the product has done in other geographic areas? Can these results be used to estimate results in Pathmark's markets?

6. *Reputation of the Company*
   Does the company have a reputation for producing winners? Do they have a strong marketing orientation? Do they have a strong retail sales force, either their own or through a full-service broker?

7. *Quality/Value Relationship*
   This is a "gatekeeper" item. If the product is not judged to provide the consumer with good value for the money, the product will not be accepted under any circumstances. Pathmark has invested too much money and time in gaining an image for selling "quality" products to jeopardize it with any item.

8. *Productivity/Labor-saving Considerations*
   Pathmark performs wholesale, transportation and retail functions that require labor and energy. Does the new product offer labor and/or energy savings opportunities? A serious negative goes to any new product that increases labor costs or energy use.

Figure 24. Continued.

SALES PRESENTATION PLANNING

The second crucial area for detailed planning in new product test marketing is in sales presentation planning. Any competent professional sales force should be capable of preparing sales presentations for existing products. The features, prices, customer reactions, etc., are all well known. This experience serves as a benchmark for preparing sales presentations. With new products, that experience base does not exist and the product development people must supply a substitute for the experience base.

Sales presentations attempt to solve a customer-product equation. For existing products, the sales force knows both sides of the equation intimately. For new products, the development group knows one half of the equation intimately—the product.

The task for the new product group in sales presentation planning is to get to know the customer and how the customer buys. In the case of consumer products, the focus of attention is the retailer or distributor who actually buys the product from you. For most industrial products, the end-user is the customer. Figures 24 and 25 will make the point clearer.

A new product that could be distributed through both types of outlets described in those Figures would have the same basic features. But a well-designed presentation would certainly stress different aspects to a Pathmark buyer than to a People's buyer. It is exactly this kind of attention to detail that is the difference between achieving distribution on schedule or not.

DISTRIBUTION PLANNING

The crucial aspect of distribution planning is developing a realistic schedule showing the rate at which distribution will be acquired. Your present product plans identify some sales level for the next period. That sales level implies a certain number of existing customers and a certain level of existing distribution. Those items don't exist for a new product.

A detailed distribution plan becomes a presentation schedule for the sales force and a production plan for the manufacturing department. Further, it is not just a question of making the sale to distributors or retailers. The key point is when the ultimate customer will be able to buy the product.

It takes six months for an average new food product in the United States to get to the point where about two-thirds of all potential customers can physically purchase the product if they wish. Drug store products take only slightly less time. Gaining distribution takes time and it is essential that your plans reflect that fact in a realistic way.

People's Drug Stores, Inc. operates about 500 drug stores. It has seven key criteria to evaluate new product offerings. While some are similar to Pathmark's criteria, others are different because they reflect differences in the operating environments of these two types of retailers.

1. *Knowledgeable Sales Force*
   Key point number one is the sales force. How knowledgeable are the sales representatives when they come to call? Does the salesman know what he's talking about?

2. *Manufacturer's Track Record*
   The track record on new products is very important. Taking on a new product represents a considerable investment for People's in money and time and being a proven winner adds a great deal of credibility.

3. *Is Product Easily Distributed and Handled?*
   Can the product go through the People's warehouse (good), or does it require store-door delivery (not so good)? Will the cases fit on our pallets? How do we know which of our stores to distribute the product to?

4. *Is it a One-Time Buy That Builds Store Traffic?*
   People's relies on certain kinds of merchandise for one-time promotions to increase store traffic.

5. *Is it a Basic or Plan-O-Gram Item?*
   Merchandise that is carried 365 days a year, basic items, all have a designated location in the store. Such designations are specified in a Plan-O-Gram, or schematic diagram, that acts as blue print for store design.

6. *Is There Adequate Lead Time Before National Advertising?*
   Generally, People's supports advertised items heavily. This requires adequate lead time for coordination, at least 12 to 16 weeks.

7. *Financial Considerations*
   Are the terms and conditions of sale, and the timing of the shipments such that People's doesn't end up in the position of financing large inventory before sales volume begins to build?

Figure 25. A drug chain's evaluation for new products

PROMOTION PLANNING

One of the fastest ways to alienate customers and discourage the sales force is to have the advertising and promotion begin before the product is available. Printing materials takes time. Producing commercials takes time. Media have lead times. Approvals take time.

You must carefully schedule all this lead time so the advertising to introduce your new product reaches the prospective customers at the same time that the product becomes available. When the lead time required to gain distribution is combined with the lead time necessary to produce and schedule promotional material, the dimensions of the planning requirements become even clearer.

HOW LONG TO TEST MARKET?

You want to be certain that you are meeting your volume goals before you make the decision to expand nationally. For consumer packaged goods and industrial supplies that rely on repeat purchases for building acceptable sales volume, determining when a new product is achieving repeat purchases equal to the volume goals is difficult.

For consumer durables and other industrial goods, the rate at which sales are being made is a little easier to assess. In all cases, you want to be certain that your crucial assumptions are confirmed.

In the final analysis, the decision to end test marketing and go into national distribution is determined by 1) how precise the test market results are and 2) how much money is risked in a national introduction versus the total profit opportunity available.

XIII

Organizing Your People for New Product Development

Without a doubt, the single most important part of a successful new product development strategy is people. All the tools, models, analyses and methods are of no value if they are being used by the wrong people, or worse, the right people in the wrong organization. Assigning the right people in the right organizational structure is the critical responsibility of top management.

There are a number of organizational forms that companies use for the new product development function. Each has its own advantages and disadvantages. Environmental considerations also have an impact on the successful development of new products. The art of management lies in selecting the right organizational form, given the best assessment of the environment, and staffing it with the most appropriate people. This section considers some of the most widely used organizational forms, some of the most important environmental considerations, and some of the characteristics of those appropriate people.

CHOOSING THE RIGHT ORGANIZATIONAL FORMS

The point of creating an organization is to be able to assign responsibilities for various tasks. The question then becomes, "Where does new product development fit in your organization? Where should the responsibility lie?" Here are some of the possible answers to that question.

The Research and Development Department: Since scientists, engineers, technicians, etc., must, in the end, be responsible for actually creating the new product, some companies locate the responsibility for new product development in the R&D department. Clearly, the people working here are in the best position to assess which accomplishments are feasible and which are not.

There are two drawbacks to assigning new product development to R&D. One is that the majority of new product failures are not technical failures, they are market failures. Since R&D personnel are not likely to be close to the market, there is a distinct possibility that products will be developed for which there is no market.

The second problem is that experience has demonstrated that R&D personnel have the longest time span view of any department in the company. It is possible that R&D will focus on products that are simply too far out into the future and not on those which can begin to produce profits in a reasonable time period.

The Marketing Department: The opposite view from R&D's lack of market orientation involves assigning new product development to the Marketing Department so as to obtain the maximum focus on the market. Fitting new product development into the Marketing Department locates the function closest to the customers in a department which should have the greatest sensitivity to customers' needs.

Experience has shown that this organizational structure also has drawbacks. The new products developed by marketing departments tend to be small and minor variations of the existing product line, i.e., one more size, a new flavor, etc. Marketing people tend to focus on very short time spans.

The other problem with this assignment is that the marketing personnel already have full-time jobs managing existing products. Even if responsibilities are re-arranged to make more time for new product work, sometimes little new product work actually gets done.

The constant pressure to manage the profitability of existing products will simply crowd out the time for new product development.

The New Product Committee: The New Product Committee combines the heads of all the departments, R&D, Marketing, Production, Finance, etc., who are eventually affected by new product development. Each department works on the part of the new product project that is most applicable, i.e., R&D does prototype development at the same time Marketing is doing the business analysis. Representatives of each department give progress reports at the New Product Committee meetings and the Committee guides the project along.

There are a lot of supposed advantages to a committee approach, including better coordination, lack of line and staff conflict, etc. The real truth is that New Product Committees do not produce new products, they only produce meetings. The line of communication from the R&D technician actually working on the project to the R&D vice president who sits on the committee to the Marketing vice president on the committee down to the Marketing analyst trying to figure out how many of these things can be sold, is very tenuous.

New Products Departments: This approach attempts to minimize the problems of the organizational structures discussed above and to maximize their advantages. A separate department is formed and staffed with a mixture of people who have the required skills and talents to develop new products. Typically, such personnel would have R&D, marketing, sales, and/or finance backgrounds. Normally you'd choose a director or vice president to head the department who has fairly broad management experience. The new products department would execute the new product development process described in this manual. It operates with plans and budgets just like any other department in the company.

New Product Departments offer many advantages. They concentrate the most appropriate skills on each task at the right time. They shorten lines of communication. They place performance in a clearly accountable position. They can be expanded or contracted in size in relation to the volume of work at hand.

Problems can develop that prevent New Product Departments from being any more effective than other forms of organization. They must compete for a share of a firm's resources. They are always in danger of being starved for resources because their activities are not immediately income-producing. New Product Departments almost always require assistance from existing departments, but frequently have very little to barter with to secure this cooperation. This is particularly true when the head of the New Product Department reports far down in the organization's chain of command.

New Product Departments can keep projects alive that really should be scrapped in order to keep department personnel busily employed. They will almost always be expensive to establish and maintain. Significant profits from new product development may well be years away and the pressures to cost justify expenses *exist today*. Finally, as the successful new products are turned over to the existing sales and marketing departments, it is easy to lose sight of the contribution originally made by the New Product Department.

Venture Teams: The very essence of new product development is starting a small business. It is one thing to start a small business on your own, but it quite another to attempt to start a new business inside a larger corporation. The reward and penalty mechanisms in large organizations tend to discourage risk-taking, which is essential to beginning business. The concept of the Venture Team is to establish a climate for entrepreneurship inside large organizations.

Usually the Venture Team concept involves assembling a small group of specialists who are assigned to develop an idea once it has passed the initial screening process. The Venture Team becomes organizationally separate from the rest of the company.

The composition of the Venture Team is likely to change as the project develops and different skills are required. In effect, personnel are "borrowed" from their regular jobs as their talents are required to move the project along. Job descriptions of the team members are vague, if they exist at all. The one constant is the assignment to bring the project to fruition. The overall objective is to assemble a group of problem-solvers with a high degree of entrepreneur orientation who will make the decisions and take the risks to get the product to market. Because of the group's autonomy, the Venture Team manager must report to an executive high up in the company structure, preferably the chief executive officer.

The real key to running successful venture teams lies in two areas. One is having a large enough pool of talented people to draw on. The other is the ability to create a climate and spirit of autonomy that encourages the Venture Team manager to take acceptable business risks.

Armour-Dial, Inc., the large Phoenix, Arizona transportation, food products and soap company attempted to establish venture teams to expedite its sluggish new product development activities. Eventually it was abandoned as a failure because it didn't produce the expected stream of new products. Team members pointed the finger of blame clearly at the president of Armour-Dial who was unwilling or unable to relinquish complete control of the workings of the various teams. He personally had to approve the smallest decision and in doing so completely robbed the team of any sense of controlling its own destiny.

ANALYZING ENVIRONMENTAL CONSIDERATIONS

Four environmental factors should be evaluated in making the decision about the kind of new product organization that best suits your requirements.

Company Size: The most important factor relates to the resources available to devote to new product development. In a small company, a one-man new product department may be the only alternative. A large, multi-divisional company may be able to afford a corporate new product department with venture teams carrying out development work within separate divisions.

One way to approach this question is to decide how much money you can afford to invest in new product development annually. Then look at what you can get for that investment. Don't just consider salaries and fringe benefits in your calculations. New product people must have money to work with to do their jobs. Travel budgets, product acquisitions, material purchases and marketing research projects are the major money needs in new product development.

As a traditional measure, if salaries exceed 50 percent of the total new product development budget, you are probably limiting the people involved and far too many decisions are being made by guessing rather than from solid field research.

Degree of Technology: In industries with a high technology base, it is very important to ensure that R&D has a high level of input in the new product development process. Rapidly changing technology always means rapidly changing markets. In these instances, the marketing people and the technical people must be able to work very closely together.

The best results occur when R&D can continually propose what the next generation of technology is likely to be, and the marketing people can continually propose how customers might be most likely to use that technology. In high technology industries, it is very easy for R&D to become the new product development focus and for the discipline of the market place to be lost.

Industry Type: The question to ask is, "How important are new products to our industry?" This is a different question than the degree of technology. New products are always important in high technology industries but they can also be very important in low technology industries. Cosmetics is a good example of an industry with a low level of technology but a very large reliance on new products for company growth. Moray Industries, the New Zealand wetsuit manufacturer, is in a low technology business, but it has made new products very important to its markets by introducing a steady stream of new styles and new features.

When new products are important in your industry, the overriding organizational consideration is fast decision-making. You must assume that some of your competitors are working on some of the same projects, and there is a premium for being first into the market with a new product.

At Moray Industries, the Managing Director and three key executives form a new product task force and make all decisions immediately. Projects move ahead quickly, or are killed just as quickly. But in either case, decisions are never delayed or postponed.

If your industry moves rapidly with new products, or if your strategy is to compete in your industry by moving rapidly with new products (as is the case with Moray Industries), you must develop an organizational structure that can produce quick decisions.

For example, a new products committee would be deadly in a rapidly moving environment. The simple problem of scheduling meetings is enough to ensure a slow decision-making process. If, however, your industry moves more slowly in introducing new products, you will have somewhat more choices in organizational form. In any case, be sure that your organizational structure can produce decisions within the necessary time frames.

Company Personality: Organizations take on a personality that reflects the aggregate personalities of its members. One way that a company takes on a personality is in regard to its attitude towards risk. Company actions then reflect that attitude towards risk.

Probably the most famous example of company attitude toward risk and that attitude's effect on the fortunes of the company can be found in Sears Roebuck & Co. and Montgomery Ward Co., the two giant retailers. At the close of World War II, the two companies were about the same size in numbers of stores and total sales and merchandise carried.

Montgomery Ward had a risk-averse management which refused to expand the business and conserved cash. Sears Roebuck's management actively accepted risk, borrowed heavily and expanded aggressively by following the mobile U.S. customers to the suburbs. The result is history. Sears is now the largest retailer in the world, and Montgomery Ward is a struggling subsidiary of the Mobil Oil Corporation.

You should make an honest assessment of your company's attitude toward risk. A risk-averse company needs an organization that can produce sufficient documentation and evidence to make risk-taking acceptable. On the other hand, a company that is more comfortable with risk-taking will profit by having a "leaner" organization and a different decision-making process. The main thing is to be sure that the organization you decide on fits the risk-taking and decision-making styles of your company.

McKinsey & Company, the international management consultants, studied the management techniques of 10 of the best managed companies in the U.S. Some serve industrial markets and some sell to consumer markets. They represented high, middle, and low technologies. Some of McKinsey's findings are particularly relevant to new product development.

In each of these highly successful companies, the management style is to "try it," then "fix it" and "try it again. " They rely heavily on controlled experiments. They avoid endless analysis and plans that appear to be complete to the tenth decimal place. They recognize that not everything they undertake will succeed. But they also realize that "paralysis by analysis" is worse.

New product development is especially vulnerable to an over-reliance on analysis and planning. That is perfectly normal. Nobody knows exactly how to do the job correctly and nobody wants to fail. An easy way out is to put off doing anything! In one major U.S. company, a new product concept has to be approved by *223* different committees before prototype development can begin. When a product fails at that company, nobody is ever responsible. But that's O.K. because they have very few products that ever get a chance to fail.

XIV

Developing Your Own Particular
New Product Strategy:
How Two Companies Did it

There are very few companies that can adopt the new product development process described in this manual in its entirety. Instead, most companies must adapt the elements of the process to fit the realities of their own situations. Now that you have a thorough understanding of how the new product development process works, your task is to analyze the operating conditions in your company and industry, and design a strategy that reflects your situation and deals most appropriately with the critical aspects of your business.

It is helpful to examine how two very different kinds of companies have addressed this task and to study how they have chosen to operate a new product development strategy that suits their needs.

Neither company is completely satisfied with its new product development system and both continually attempt to improve. These two examples are not meant to be blueprints for your system. They do, however, provide you with some insights about how other executives have faced the same problems and the kinds of decisions that resulted.

THE CASE OF WIENERSCHNITZEL, INC.

Wienerschnitzel is a fast food chain headquartered in Newport Beach, California. Wienerschnitzel was founded after World War II along with McDonald's, Kentucky Fried Chicken and other fast food franchising operations. While McDonald's created a market position for itelf with hamburgers and Kentucky Fried Chicken with chicken, Wienerschnitzel specialized in serving hot dogs. Its menu included just about every way that a hot dog can be served individually as a sandwich.

By the late 1970's, Wienerschnitzel was operating, or had franchised, about 350 such "hot dog stores" in 11 Western states. Although Wienerschnitzel is privately owned and does not publicly disclose operating results, total sales were in excess of $100 million.

Management, however, found that it faced declining sales and real cash flow problems. It had no serious new product development strategy or program. In an effort to directly attack this problem of stagnant growth, Wienerschnitzel assembled a team of its top operating executives and assigned the task of developing a new product strategy and then executing it successfully.

ESTABLISHING GUIDELINES

The first task that the team addressed was an analysis of the company's strengths and weaknesses. Out of this activity the team developed a definition of the business that it chose to be in. This business definition provided the guidelines for future new product development.

> A custom-prepared, sandwich-oriented, non-plastic restaurant offering full service restaurant food quality with fast food prices, speed, and convenience.

This business definition eliminates a wide variety of new products that the team might have pursued and at the same time sets criteria for the kinds of new products that would be acceptable.

GENERATING IDEAS

The first step that the team took to generate new product ideas was to conduct an in-depth study of the market for fast food. The second step was to analyze the company's capabilities to fill unmet customer needs. These activities narrowed the focus of the new product idea search. The major findings were:

- In its marketing areas, Wienerschnitzel held very high market shares, 80 percent to 90 percent, of the market for hot dogs eaten away from home.

- The total market for hot dogs eaten away from home was not very big and showed no signs of growth.

- The sales slump at Wienerschnitzel was also occurring at the other major fast food chains. The fundamental reason for this was that the 18 to 34 year-olds who had provided the basis for much of the growth in the fast food business during the 1950's and 1960's had changed their eating away from home behavior.

- Significant numbers of the target market, young adults from 18 to 34 years old, had upgraded the environment surrounding their away from home eating. They now favored pub-like theme restaurants and indoor sit-down restaurants, usually with extended menus and beer and wine service.

- In spite of the expanded menus offered in the new pubs, hamburgers, regular and a half dozen variations, accounted for as much as 90 percent of the food orders.

The team concluded that Wienerschnitzel had to find additional menu items to attract some of the target market back from the pubs, or face a bleak future.

SCREENING CONCEPTS

In addition to the guidelines for new product development, the team decided that any item considered must meet two additional criteria; 1) it should have a bigger profit margin that hot dogs and, 2) it should not require a major investment in equipment by the franchise operators.

The team decided that the following items were worth consideration:

- A prepared dessert consisting of a cake or graham cracker base with a layer of flavor filling and a whipped topping.
- A breakfast menu consisting of an egg sandwich, Danish pastry, juice and coffee.
- A one-third pound hamburger
- A fish sandwich and a fish platter
- A steak sandwich

COMBINING STEPS

Business analysis, prototype development and limited store testing all took place virtually simultaneously. The key elements in the business analysis were a) the effects of each of the test products on production capability in individual stores, and b) the incremental income produced vis-a-vis the amount of money required to advertise and promote the new products.

Product specifications can be prepared in test kitchens, but the majority of the prototype development must take place in the stores since the ability of basically unskilled young people to prepare the food items is as important as the ingredients themselves.

Prototype development concentrated on getting customer reactions to the various food items as they are actually served in test stores at various price levels. This is the point where Wienerschnitzel spent the bulk of the available marketing research funds. The ability of the products to satisfy customers and to generate business is the crucial measurement.

Prototype development begins with limited store testing, typically five stores. Once a new product has successfully passed business analysis and prototype development, full comercialization can be accomplished fairly easily. The primary consideration is advertising media coverages, since all Wienerschnitzel stores in a media market must be able and ready to deliver the advertised product. Thus, Wienerschnitzel can roll out a new product introduction on a market-by-market basis, or introduce the product throughout its 11 state marketing area all at once.

The careful development of a new product strategy and the ensuing successful execution of that strategy has paid off for Wienerschnitzel. Total sales in 1983 will exceed $150 million and virtually all of the increase is due to sales from newly developed and introduced products.

Figure 26 shows how the company approached the business analysis and prototype development planning for the one new concept.

SMITH INTERNATIONAL, INC.

Smith International, Inc. is also headquartered in Newport Beach, California, but is very different from Wienerschnitzel. First of all, Smith is 10 times bigger than Wienerschnitzel and had total revenues in 1981 of over $1 billion. Second. Smith sells to industrial markets and is a leading manufacturer and worldwide marketer of premium quality products and services for use in oil and gas field drilling and in mining.

There are two other features that are markedly different. Smith has nine separate divisions and had to deal with explosive growth during the 1970's. Revenues tripled from 1977 to 1981 alone.

Smith International, Inc. manages its multiple divisions and rapid growth by careful attention to strategic planning. Its plans mark the direction for the total company and set goals for the individual divisions. One of those divisions is Tungsten Carbide Manufacturing.

The Tungsten Carbide group was originally started by Smith in the early 1970's to supply the cutting teeth inserts for Smith drill bits. By the end of the 1970's, Tungsten Carbide had been set up as a separate profit center, selling products to the parent company, but also trying to build a sales base outside the Smith International divisions.

Tungsten Carbide has adapted the new product development process to fit its own particular requirements and industry structure. Manufacturing and marketing the world's hardest abrasive materials is certainly different from Wienerschnitzel's business, but the new product development process is very similar.

FISH SANDWICH AND PLATTER

Objective
The objective is to determine the operational compatibility and consumer acceptance of a fish sandwich and platter.

The Product
The products that will be tested are:

1. *Fish Sandwich*
   2.5 ounce, irregularly shaped, batter dipped cod fillet that is deep fried and served on a toasted bun with .75 ounces of tarter sauce and 2.5 ounces of lettuce.

2. *Fish Platter*
   Two 2.5 ounce, irregularly shaped, batter dipped cod fillet, deep fired, served with 2.5 ounces of french fries and one ounce cup of tarter sauce and, under consideration, a sprig of parsley on an oval platter.

Rationale
The decision to test this product was based on the following:

- These particular products were very successful at Gino's, where the sandwich increased sales by 5% and the platter by 5%.
- Research shows that heavy users of McDonald's fish sandwiches prefer this product.
- Both of these items carry a very low food cost and should help to lower the overall food cost of our units.

Test Stores
The fish sandwich and platters will be tested in two stores; Unit #287 in Tustin and #150 in Long Beach.

Strategies
A. *Pricing*
   The fish sandwich will be sold for 79 cents and the platter for $1.69. These prices are based on food costs and competitive pricing information.

Figure 26. A real new product analysis plan

B. *Advertising*

For the testing stage of new product development, point of purchase materials will be used to create awareness and trial.

C. *Packaging*

The sandwich will be served wrapped in paper, and the fish platter will be served on a platter for dining room consumption and in a clam shell container for take-out.

Food Costs

The food costs for the fish sandwich and platter are:

Fish Sandwich		Fish Platter	
Fish	.22	Fish	.44
Tarter Sauce	.033	Tarter Sauce	.033
Wrap	.008	Fries	.08
Lettuce	.007	Platter	.032
Bun	.05	Cup for Sauce	.034
Total	.318	Lemon Wedge	.012
Price	.79	Total	.0631
Food Cost in %: 40.25%		Price	1.69
		Food Cost in %: 37.3%	

Data Analysis

The following data will be collected and analyzed:

- Product Sales Mix
- Ideal Food Costs
- Food Wastage
- Sales Data
- Labor Cost
- Speed of Service—Average Transaction Time
- Trial and Repeat

The above data will be assembled and used to decide whether or not to proceed with a test market.

Figure 26. Continued

ESTABLISHING GUIDELINES

Good strategic planning begins with the development of a mission statement, a description of the company and what it wishes to become. The existence of a well-formulated strategic plan provides most of the guidelines to direct new product development.

This is exactly what happens at Smith International. It has developed mission statements for each of the operating companies, as well as an overall corporate mission statement. Each of the divisions' mission statements are compatible with and complementary to the overall corporate statement.

Tungsten Carbide's mission statement directs the group toward excellence in abrasives and reflects the division's dual role as an in-house supplier and as a competitor in the general market place. Figure 27 shows the Smith and Tungsten Carbide statements.

GENERATING IDEAS

The market is segmented into three distinct parts in terms of the depth of the well being drilled. Type I wells are relatively shallow and not very complex in their requirements. Type II wells are those drilled to intermediate depths and require more complex equipment and services. Type III wells are drilled to the greatest depths, often under adverse environmental conditions at the drilling site, and must deal with extremely high underground pressures and temperatures. Tungsten Carbide attempts to generate ideas for new product concepts in these three market segments. To do this, they use three general methods.

One method is to continually canvass the other Smith divisions for products that are currently being purchased outside the company that Tungsten Carbide could supply with either better quality or price.

The second method is competitive analysis. Tungsten Carbide personnel are regular trade show visitors with instructions to develop a complete list of products manufactured by competitors. Since the U.S. market alone is over $1 billion annually for the kinds of products that Tungsten Carbide manufactures, and since there are over 50 com-

Corporate Mission Statement

Smith International is a leading manufacturer and worldwide marketer of premium quality products and services whose performance enhances productivity for customers in drilling, completion and production of oil and gas wells, and in mining.

Our strength derives from the added value we provide to meet the critical economic and technical needs of the markets Smith International serves.

Smith International's strategic path is marked by continued, lateral diversification of performance-oriented products and services across increasingly broader segments of the petroleum service and mining industries.

Division Mission Statement

Tungsten Carbide is in business to supply wear resistant materials such as carbides, cermets or ceramics. The primary mission is to supply these materials and services which will achieve maximum performance for Smith International products.

The mission also includes increasing financial returns to Smith International stockholders. This will be achieved by obtaining an acceptable long-term Return on Total Capital (ROTC) through profitably expanding internal and external sales. This growth will keep Tungsten Carbide on the leading edge of technology. However, strategies may require investments that would negatively affect the financial returns to Tungsten Carbide but still be investments that are in the best interest of Smith International.

Figure 27. Two compatible mission statements

petitors, this kind of competitive analysis is a valuable source of new product ideas.

As the third method, Tungsten Carbide uses its sales force to continually survey its customers to identify unmet needs. This survey activity is formally structured and relies on a questionnaire developed at Tungsten Carbide's headquarters and shown in Figure 28.

SCREENING IDEAS

In addition to meeting the criteria set out in the mission statement for the division, each new product idea must meet three financial criteria as well. These financial criteria are consistent with the parent corporation's mission statement, " . . . we believe that cash flow is the best single measure of economic success. Cash is the economic return valued most by our investors and creditors." Accordingly, corporate management has established goals for 1) cash flow, 2) return on assets and 3) net operating profit after taxes that are used as screening criteria.

BUSINESS ANALYSIS

The *crucial* step in the new product development process at Tungsten Carbide is the business analysis because actual prototype development costs are so high. To deal with this fact, Tungsten Carbide has developed a build-up estimating model similar to the one shown in Section X. Tungsten Carbide's estimating model has just three components in order to focus attention clearly on the most critical aspects of the business analysis.

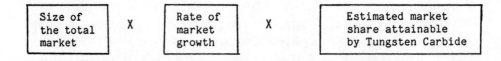

Three sources of data are generally used to estimate the first two components, market size and market growth rate. One is an on-line computer data base provided by an outside supplier. This data base gives Tungsten Carbide immediate access to a wide variety of secondary source market data. The second source of data is non-custom studies by marketing research companies which specialize in secondary source research.

When no applicable. reliable or usable data can be found in the computer data bank, and when no studies are available, Tungsten Carbide uses its third source and commissions custom research projects from an outside research firm.

(All questions refer to your specific sales area)

1. What is the 1982 total monetary market for *(new product)* in your area?

2. What sizes will be the most popular and how many pieces by size will your customers buy, in total, in 1982? (monetary amount and pieces)

3. Who are the major competitors for (new product) in your area and what portion of the market do they hold? (percent and monetary amount)

4. Can you obtain competition price lists for all of these competitors?

5. What are the end uses for *(new product)* in your sales area?

6. What industries will be most affected by the use of (new product)?

7. What product qualities do customers look for in *(new product)*?

8. What other sources would be useful in obtaining marketing information on *(new product)*?

Figure 28. A typical questionnaire for a Tungsten salesperson

The third component of the estimating model is provided by Tungsten Carbide's top management. After examining all the data available, and after reviewing the company's record in competing in similar market situations, a judgment is made about the most likely share of market that the company could attain.

PROTOTYPE DEVELOPMENT

There really are no separate steps for prototype development and commercialization at Tungsten Carbide. Machine tooling costs make up the great bulk of the development product costs and they are simply not divisible. Therefore, Tungsten Carbide usually moves directly from business analysis to full commercialization.

When a project successfully passes business analysis, sales materials are prepared and the sales force is requested to obtain an order from a prospective customer. At that point, the production department goes to work and Tungsten Carbide has a new product.

FINAL COMMENTS

A quick look at these two quite different companies might lead you to think that they developed new products in different ways. This would not be an accurate assessment.

Both companies follow the steps in the new product development process very carefully. Each company has adapted the process to meet its own requirements. Each has developed a system that concentrates the greatest attention on the most crucial aspects of the process for its environment.

Wienerschnitzel focuses on consumer reaction to its new products because capital spending *is not* very important and customer attitudes toward the company's restaurants *are* very important. Accordingly, it spends the bulk of its funds and attention on prototype development.

On the other hand, Tungsten Carbide takes greatest care with the business analysis part of the new product development process. A new product that passes business analysis will require an immediate expenditure of at least $10,000 and maybe as much as $100,000. The company wisely focuses its funds and attention on minimizing the risk that such tooling costs will be lost.

It is unlikely that either of these systems will completely suit your requirements. But somewhere between hot dogs and drill bit inserts there is a new product development strategy and system that will produce the kinds of sales and profits you need.

Appendix

A. C. NIELSEN COMPANY OFFICES

U.S.A.
Nielsen Plaza
Northbrook, Illinois 60062

62 Perimeter Center East, N.E.
Atlanta, Georgia 30346

40 William Street
Wellesley, Massachusetts 02181

Barclay Pavilion, Route 70
Cherry Hill, New Jersey 08034

410 North Michigan Avenue
Chicago, Illinois 60611

333 West Campbell Road, Suite 350
Richardson, Texas 75080

211 Grandview Drive
Fort Mitchell, Kentucky 41017

401 Hackensack Avenue, Continental Plaza
Hackensack, New Jersey 07601

70 Willow Road
Menlo Park, California 94025

1290 Avenue of the Americas
New York, New York 10104

830 Post Road East
Westport, Connecticut 06880

OVERSEAS
A. C. Nielsen Pty. Limited
50 Miller Street
North Sidney, N. S. W.
Australia

A. C. Nielsen Company, Ges.m.b.H.
Concordiaplatz, 2
1013 Vienna 1, Austria

A. C. Nielsen Company (Belgium) S. A.
Avenue des Arts, 56, B-1040
Brussels, Belgium

A. C. Nielsen Company (French Branch)
28 Boulevard de Grenelle
75737 Paris Cedex 15
France

A. C. Nielsen Company, G.m.b.H.
Friedrich-Ebert-Anlage 2–14
P.O. Box 16580
6000 Frankfurt AM Main
FRG

A. C. Nielsen (Nederland) B. V.
Amsteldijki 166
1079 LH Amsterdam
P.O. Box 7000
1007 MA
Amsterdam, Netherlands

A. C. Nielsen (N. Z.) Limited
Molesworth House
Molesworth Street
Wellington, New Zealand

A. C. Nielsen Company (Spanish Branch)
Luchana 23-6
P.O. Box 10149
Madrid 10, Spain

A. C. Nielsen Company
Storholmsgaten 11, 2nd Floor
Skarholmen, Sweden

A. C. Nielsen S. A.
Nielsen House
Buchrain/Lucerne
Switzerland

A. C. Nielsen Company Limited
Nielsen House
Headington, Oxford OX 9RX
England

CANADA
A. C. Nielsen Company of Canada Limited
160 McNab Street, Markham,
Ontario. Canada L3R 4B8

100 Alexis Hihon Boulevard, Suite 280
St. Laurent, P. Q. Canada H4M 2N7

1200 West 73rd Avenue, Suite 501
Vancouver, B. C., Canada V6P 6G5

Index

Page numbers in **bold** indicate information
found in tables and figures.